CIVIL DEATH IN NEW YORK STATE

How New York State Utiliizes Criminal
Conviction Records to impede the Economic
Growth of Formerly Convicted People

ERIC M. DEADWILEY

IUNIVERSE, INC.
NEW YORK   BLOOMINGTON

CIVIL DEATH IN NEW YORK STATE
How New York State Utiliizes Criminal Conviction Records to impede the Economic Growth of Formerly Convicted People

iUniverse books may be ordered through booksellers or by contacting:

iUniverse
1663 Liberty Drive
Bloomington, IN 47403
www.iuniverse.com
1-800-Authors (1-800-288-4677)

Because of the dynamic nature of the Internet, any Web addresses or links contained in this book may have changed since publication and may no longer be valid.

ISBN: 978-1-4401-9473-3 (sc)
ISBN: 978-1-4401-9472-6 (ebk)

Library of Congress Control Number: 2009912439

Printed in the United States of America

iUniverse rev. date: 12/14/2009

CONTENTS

INTRODUCTION

Unemployment is at crisis levels in New York's Black communities. This crisis is largely due to institutional racism and state sponsored discrimination. The United States has over 16 million convicted people, and that number grows each year. The nation runs the risk of criminalizing an entire racial group in the coming years. Blacks are arrested, prosecuted, convicted, and incarcerated at much higher rates than other ethnic groups. Civil death penalties are crippling Black communities. Unless policies are changed to remove the social stigma on people with criminal convictions; we will see a further depletion of the Black family unit in the coming years.

Images depicting young Black males as criminals, rapists, and drug dealers are broadcasted daily on television and radios. This book will provide a better understanding of how civil death penalties affect Black families. The legitimate need for employers to know the criminal background of potential employees must be weighed against the interests of the innocent children, families, and communities of the formerly convicted.

DEDICATION

I want to give special thanks to almighty God for giving me the order to write this book. This book is also dedicated to my wife, Gardenia, our children, and my mother, Lillian, for all of their support throughout my studies.

CHAPTER

1

THE HISTORY OF CIVIL DEATH
PENALTIES IN AMERICA

Two widely recognized phrases used by politicians and social scholars in reference to civil death penalties (civil death penalties are legal restrictions to housing, employment and licensure on people with criminal convictions) are "collateral consequences" and "felony disenfranchisement." *Disenfranchisement* is defined in Webster's Collegiate Dictionary as "The denial of a right or privilege granted to other persons or groups" (Webster, 1983). The term "felony disenfranchisement" is often used by scholars, civil rights advocates, and politicians to describe the legal loss of a person's right to vote.

Many people believe that the right to vote is the most essential right a citizen possesses. The right to vote is one of our more fundamental and vital civil rights. However, many Blacks do not believe that the right to vote is the most important civil right. Only if Blacks enjoyed truly equal protection under the law could the right to vote be the most important right; as it pertains to civil rights. Laws are only as strong as those who are entrusted to enforce them.

To people with criminal convictions, disenfranchisement means much more than just the loss of the right to vote. "Civil Death Penalties, known as felony disenfranchisement laws in America, actually were Greek and Roman customs carried over into Europe" (Pinkerton, 2002).

These penalties were referred to as civil death, and were actually punishments. The purpose of civil death penalties was to deter crime by publicly humiliating criminals. These penalties were also designed to punish the families of criminal offenders. A convicted person's right to vote was taken away.

According to Pinkerton:

> Any such offenses were punishable before the town people. This was a method of shaming the wrongdoer, so they would not commit the act again. Generally adulterers were forced to wear the letter "A" sewed on their clothes and counterfeiters wore the letter "C". Others might have their ears clipped or actually be branded. Public executions were regularly attended by thousands of people among them women and children.

These forms of punishments were designed to let the public "join in" the punishment process of offenders. This caused the person who committed the offense to be segregated from society. The person's family was also ostracized. The film *The Scarlet Letter* chronicled the punishment of a married woman convicted of adultery (Joffe, 1995). The woman is forced to wear a large letter "A" on her clothing to signify her conviction. Letters are no longer sewn on a formerly convicted person's clothing, and civil death is no longer confined to just a small village or township. A conviction is now branded on a person's public biography, which can be electronically disseminated all across the world.

Ancient Europeans openly practiced some of the cruelest forms of punishment that man has ever witnessed. Under the watch of the Catholic Church's Inquisition, thousands of people were tortured, burned alive, hung by the neck, decapitated, dismembered, or flogged. These atrocities, masquerading as justice, were often done in the presence of cheering crowds. In the film *Hang 'Em High*, Clint Eastwood portrays a lawman in search of the men who hung him and left him to die. The territory he (Clint Eastwood) patroled was judged by a man who hung the defendants in the town square while cheering town folk watched (T. Post , 1968).

Another popular movie which reference civil death penalties is *March of the Wooden Soldiers* (Rogers, 1934). Two toymakers, portrayed by Stan Laurel and Oliver Hardy, were convicted of burglary. As a result, they were locked in the stocks, sentenced to the ducking stool (strapped in a chair and dunked underwater), then "banished to Bogeyland." All of this was done in the middle of town while the citizenry watched.

The Inquisition used many methods of torture and execution to maintain the moral principles of the Church. This may be the reason why employers use moral character as a reason for not employing people with criminal convictions. Even if a formerly convicted person abides all laws for a decade or more after incarceration or conviction, and clearly demonstrates that they are truly rehabilitated, employers still have the right under New York state law to use a prior criminal conviction as justification for denying employment. Many agencies compiling statistical data on the formerly convicted conclude that the longer a person with a criminal conviction remains a law-abiding citizen, the less likely the chances of their offending again. Thus the criminal background information eventually becomes illegitimate, unreasonable, and unnecessary to employers. Many employers are simply utilizing the information to practice personal discriminatory beliefs.

CHAPTER

2

SHOULD EMPLOYERS ALWAYS HAVE THE RIGHT TO REQUEST CRIMINAL BACKGROUND INFORMATION?

Most employers feel they have a legitimate right to know whether prospective hires have ever been convicted of a crime. This question appears on most job applications: *Have you ever been convicted of a crime*? This question is used to sift out applicants thought to be undesirable. This question, which New York and many other states allow employers to ask perspective employees, should be restricted to a definite period of time, and should have limited use on public-sector employment applications.

There is an undeniable stigma associated with any person with a criminal record. Former offenders are labeled by the media and politicians as ex-cons, convicts, criminals, or felons. Criminal background information should be expunged after a definite period of time based on the seriousness of the offense and the sincerity of rehabilitation efforts.

It is not in the best interests of society to continue the use of past criminal offenses as a predictor of how a person would perform in a job. The empirical data suggest that after a given period of time has passed from a person's conviction or release from incarceration, that person presents no more of a risk than someone without a criminal background (Kurlychek, Brame, and Bushway, 2006). The social stigma of a criminal conviction stifles the progress of millions of Americans in obtaining gainful employment *for life*, or at least long after they have completed their sentence and have desisted from committing criminal acts. Some politicians (Aubry, 2009) have recently acknowledged that employers openly discriminate against people with criminal convictions.

New York State Assemblyman Jeffrion Aubry, 2006, a Democrat, is a longtime proponent of criminal justice reform. Assemblyman Aubry recently introduced a bill to amend laws related to the conditional sealing of drug convictions (Bill #A5633). Aubry's justification for the bill is as follows:

> Thousands of New Yorkers currently must deal with the stigma associated with having a criminal record for the rest of their lives as they seek employment and housing and strive to become productive members of society – even after they have fully paid their debt to society and, in many cases, lived law-abiding lives for many years after completion of their sentences.

> New York State has long been a leader in providing fair employment opportunities for qualified individuals with criminal histories for the sensible reason that people with criminal records who are able to earn a living are much more likely to lead productive, tax-paying lives and much less likely to return to crime ... Recognizing the wisdom of assisting individuals with criminal records who are qualified and not a threat to public safety to obtain employment and housing, a wide range of leaders, including a diverse group convened by former Mayor Ed Koch in 1989, and Governor Pataki when he proposed his drug law reform bill of 2003, have proposed that New York State enact a law to permit the sealing of certain nonviolent criminal records.

> This bill is designed to allow people convicted of nonviolent drug offenses that have completed appropriate treatment and/or remained crime-free an opportunity to rebuild their lives without the stigma of a criminal record.

Many people with criminal convictions have abided by the law for years, even decades after paying their debt to society. Yet, they are still subjected to this question when seeking employment. The crime a person has committed can *never* change. This is the primary contradiction inherent in civil death penalties, as well as the contradiction in Aubry's bill. No amount of incarceration serves to satisfy the debt, no matter what the offender's age was at the time of the offense, no matter how much change a person with a criminal conviction could have made in their lives since the crime and punishment. Formerly convicted people must *publicly* carry around that crime as a part of their credentials forever. Imagine if a HIV-positive person had to reveal that fact every time they applied for a job. Would this be reasonable, or even legally defensible?

Civil death penalties are not considered to be a direct part of a crime and punishment. Judges, prosecutors, and defense attorneys do not explain to criminal defendants at sentencing that they will be automatically barred from one half of the available gainful employment in the United States. Furthermore, formerly convicted people will likely face discrimination by those employers who do not automatically reject them. If such notifications were standard, there would not be so many plea bargains accepted. The healthcare industry, law enforcement agencies, armed forces, licensed professional fields, airline industry, financial industry, and many other private-sector industries will not hire people with criminal convictions as a rule.

Most city and state jobs are also unavailable to people with criminal convictions, for reasons of safety or unreasonable risk. Additionally, civil death penalties have done nothing at all in terms of deterring crime and protecting the community. The only real accomplishment these penalties achieve is to amplify the punishment of a formerly convicted person's sentence, a domino effect that adversely affects families as well.

Recent statistics put unemployment of Black males at an all time high. A recent Community Service Society study showed Blacks have the highest unemployment of any ethnic group in New York City (Levitan, 2007).

President Barack Obama gave a press conference on the occasion of his first 100 days in office. At this press conference, he was asked the following question by a Black Entertainment Television reporter:

> As the entire nation tries to climb out of this deep recession, in communities of color, the circumstances are far worse. The Black unemployment rate, as you know, is in the double digits. And in New York City, for example, the Black unemployment rate for men is near 50 percent. My question to you tonight is, given this unique and desperate circumstance, what specific policies can you point to that will target these communities, and what's the timetable for us to see tangible results?

President Obama stated:

> Well, keep in mind that every step we're taking is designed to help all people. But folks who are most vulnerable are most likely to be helped because they need the most help ... So my general approach is that if the economy is strong, that will lift all boats as long as it is also supported by, for example, strategies around college affordability and job training, tax cuts

for working families as opposed to the wealthiest, that will level the playing field and ensure bottom-up economic growth" (*Huffington Post*, 2009).

Economists and politicians seem to be scratching their heads in disbelief at New York City Blacks unemployment, underemployment, and job loss. Politicians seem reluctant to understand and denounce civil death penalties as one of the main causes of Black male unemployment.

The Rockefeller drug laws and three-strike legislation have filled New York's correctional facilities with young Black and Hispanic people. Civil death penalties, along with weak civil rights laws, have fueled a surge in unemployment of young Black Americans. Many people are now seeing the connections between Black male unemployment rates and criminal convictions. These connections are not hidden. The same legislators that make the laws openly admit that the social stigma of a criminal conviction is a debilitating factor for job seekers.

The FBI, the federal government's Department of Justice, and New York's Department of Correctional Services compile yearly statistics on crime and incarceration. The Department of Justice compiles yearly data on the United States prison population. Presently there are several academic institutions, governmental agencies, and non-profits that compile data and conduct studies into the social and economic problems civil death penalties (also known as felony disenfranchisement laws and collateral consequences) impose on citizens with criminal convictions. We need to have a better understanding of how these laws affect our nation's economy, social structure, community safety, prison population and family life.

Regardless of the term by which you refer to these statutes and policies (formal or informal), they are unacceptably discriminatory. This discrimination excessively impacts Blacks particularly in New York but also around the country. This is a clear violation of Title VII of the Civil Rights Act of 1964.

Civil rights leaders, academics, and social scholars speak out about the injustice of civil death penalties and the disenfranchisement of people with criminal convictions, yet even these sympathetic advocates limit the scope of "disenfranchisement" to merely the loss of one's right to vote. "Felony disenfranchisement" and "civil death penalties" are undoubtedly one and the same, and should be categorized as such. Civil death penalties are not direct penalties related to sentences and punishments given by courts. However, the sentencing judges, prosecutors and defense attorney's follow the same laws manufactured by the state legislators that created civil death penalties. This is why, to some degree, there is double jeopardy being imposed on rehabilitated people with criminal convictions. In New York, criminal procedure law and corrections law are manufactured by the very same entity, the State Legislature.

Our leaders variously refer to people with criminal convictions as convicts, ex-cons, hardened criminals, and felons, as if a letter is branded on the heads of citizens who have criminal convictions. This is no coincidence: Branding was used to punish criminal offenders by the Greeks and Romans. Corporal punishment in those days also involved floggings, beatings, mutilations, blinding and the use of the stock or pillory (*Encyclopedia Britannica*, 2009).

A columnist in the *New York Daily News* (referring to Assemblyman Aubry's bill) wrote:

> Under this statute—part of a larger rollback of penalties for drug crimes—courts will start sealing the records of certain drug-related criminals, effectively wiping the slate clean when they apply for jobs ... Which will be cold comfort for the family that discovers too late that they have entrusted their baby to a former Crack-head (Hammond, 2009).

In this column, Bill Hammond insidiously used his power as a media commentator to plant the seeds of fear by highlighting one of the world's most sensitive occupations, babysitting. Hammond's manipulative statement is a perfect example why these laws must be eradicated.

There are many books, reports, and articles about the civil death penalties formerly convicted people face. Statistics provide additional proof that civil death penalties are unjust, that successfully rehabilitated former criminal offenders should not be stricken with lifelong restrictions to employment and other services. These laws could be ruled unconstitutional given the empirical data debunking their effectiveness. Title VII of the Civil Rights Act of 1964 makes it illegal for a law, practice, or policy to disparately impact any group where there is no business necessity for that particular law, practice, or policy. Empirical data shows that after seven to ten years, the formerly convicted commit crimes at similar rates as non-offenders (Kurlychek *et al*, 2006).

People often make generalizations regarding what crimes the criminal justice system should have leniency on. The consensus is that minor drug crimes should be dealt with by creating alternatives to incarceration. There also seems to be a growing consensus that incarceration should be reserved for those who commit violent crimes. Our state's scarce prison resources should be used for those offenders who are in no way rehabilitated, and certainly not for first-time drug offenders. However, no one should minimize illegal drug's adverse impact on low-income minority communities.

Many urban residents remember living in a siege state thanks to drug dealers. Who do you think purchased, owned and used semiautomatic and automatic weapons before violent crime declined in recent years? Far too many people have fallen victim to senseless acts of violence related to drug turf disputes. There is an ongoing discussion on treatment programs as an alternative to incarceration for minor narcotics offenses.

According to a 2002 New York State Department of Correctional Services three-year post-release follow-up, 73 percent of freed drug offenders released were actually convicted for selling drugs. Those convicted of trafficking were more likely to return than people sentenced for possession by a measure of 42 percent to 31 percent.

In the motion picture *Scarface*, Al Pacino played a narcotics trafficker who was warned by a drug lord "Don't get high on your own supply." Most drug dealers are not users, and most dealers do not use addicts to sell their drugs; this would be tantamount to hiring *Sesame*

Street's Cookie Monster as a security guard at the Chips Ahoy Factory. Many organizations and advocates of people with criminal convictions are not of the opinion that only nonviolent offenders should be given a second chance. The policy of permanent public scrutiny of past criminal records has failed. We can no longer continue classifying all drug crimes as equal.

Just as all drug crimes are not equivalent, the same scenario also applies to violent crimes. Most violent crimes do not involve actual physical violence, merely the threat of violence. Yet politicians used the very realistic fears of citizens tired of rampant violence in the early nineties to pass sweeping legislation that enacted stiffer penalties for violent offenses. "Tough on Crime" was the order of the day politically. Civil Death Penalties mostly affect minority communities.

Some politicians built their careers on tough-on-crime politics. Former New York State Governor George E. Pataki was elected on such a platform. The very moment Pataki took office, his Executive Order #5 was implemented. This order denied work release to any prisoner in New York State correctional facilities with a violent offense on their record. Politicians often use well-publicized crimes to justify draconian policies.

Pataki ran his entire campaign on anti-violent crime rhetoric. One of the incidents that Pataki often cited to justify his call for tough anti-crime measures was the 2000 "Wendy's Massacre." Two Black men murdered five employees of a Wendy's fast food restaurant. The victims were bound, gagged and shot execution-style in the basement of the restaurant. Former New York

City Mayor Rudolph Giuliani utilized tough-on-crime political posturing and policy as well.

Most advocates of people with criminal convictions do not have a problem with tough-on-crime policies. This is probably due to their belief that punishment should be proportional to the nature of the crime. However, growing numbers of reform advocates do believe that there should be a time limit on criminal records. If not expunged, then there should be a specific length of time since conviction or release that the details of a person's past criminal record should be accessible to law enforcement officials only. Cloaking punishment as a mere collateral consequence is an insidious, malevolent policy that hurts families. Furthermore, these extended sentences damage communities for generations. What are innocent children supposed to do when their parents are denied employment for crimes committed before they were even born? How is such a secondary impact seen as reasonable?

CHAPTER

3

WHY UNRESTRICTED CIVIL DEATH PENALTIES ARE NOT IN THE BEST INTERESTS OF SOCIETY

There is evidence that racism is so pervasive, so institutionalized in our society that Black citizens seeking employment in New York cannot get fair treatment.

A recent study by Princeton sociologists found that "discrimination has not been eliminated in the post-civil rights period as some contend, but remains a vital component of a complex pattern of racial inequality" (Pager and Western, 2005).

The 2004 study, titled "Race at Work: Realities of Race and Criminal Record in the NYC Job Market," sent well-qualified young Black, white, and Latino men to apply for 1,470 low-paying entry-level jobs throughout New York City. The study uncovered a current dynamic of discrimination based on race and national origin. The first set of results was derived from a three-person team (comprised of white, Black, and Latino males ranging in age from twenty-two to twenty-six) who applied for the same positions and presented similar credentials. The investigation also found that Latinos were preferred over their Black counterparts. Recent trends in hiring shows Latinos to be the preferred ethnic group. In addition, the Princeton study found that white applicants with felony convictions appear to do just as well (if not better) than Blacks with no criminal background. The report concludes that "despite the fact that these applicants presented equivalent credentials and applied for exactly the same jobs, race appears to overtake all else in determining employment opportunities."

In another study, "The Mark of a Criminal Record," it was posited that "criminal records close doors in employment situations". This research took place in Milwaukee, Wisconsin. The study found that "Blacks are less than half as likely to receive consideration by employers, relative to their white counterparts, and black non-offenders fall behind even whites with prior felony convictions" (Pager, 2003).

Most comprehensive studies on the effects that race and criminal conviction status have on employment opportunities conclude that race in and of itself play a major role in hiring practices in all sectors.

On January 22, 2007, in the 110th Congress, first Session, Congressman Charles Rangel introduced House Resolution 623, "The Second Chance Act of 2007." In his address Rangel spoke directly to the need to help the 16 million ex-felons currently living in the United States. The congressman spoke passionately on the need for a second chance for nonviolent offenders who have paid their debt to society. Rangel made the argument that "a second chance is needed for nonviolent people with criminal convictions because of the inherent problems they have finding employment and all of the sanctions placed on people with criminal convictions, particularly (nonviolent) drug offenders" (Rangel, 2007).

We should all be concerned with politicians who believe that such a highly discriminated-against group as formerly convicted people should be split into two groups as it pertains to a second chance to feed their families. The rationale for Congressman Rangel's bill is to allow people with criminal convictions a second chance at life, a chance to regain the status they held before their offense. But Rangel would only give nonviolent former offenders that chance. Should violent offenders have to forever deal with these barriers to employment and a normal life?

The Milwaukee study found that violent offenders were treated more unfavorably by employers compared to drug offenders. The barriers set before drug offenders, which bar them from public housing, receiving food stamps, and federal educational funding, are totally unjust approaches to dealing with their crimes. However, the statistics do not support the confidence that most supporters of Rangel-style legislation have that nonviolent offenders will not offend again. In fact, the statistics show felony drug offenders have the highest recidivism rates in New York State.

The New York State Department of Correctional Services' own findings suggest that violent offenders returned at lower rates. "Among offenders who were re-committed for a new felony offense, the most frequent crime where re-commitments occurred was drug offenses,

up to a 41 percent return rate within three years"
(NYSDOCS, 2002).

According to the United States Census Bureau
(USCB), there were 36 million Blacks and 37 million
Hispanics in the United States in 2002 (USCB, 2003).
It is estimated that there are over 16 million people with
criminal convictions in the United States. Many advocates believe that 16 million is a gross underestimate, and
the true figure is closer to 25 million.

According to the National Criminal Justice Reference
Service: "Nearly 81 million individual offenders were in
the criminal history files of the state criminal history repositories on December 31, 2006" (National Consortium
for Justice Information and Statistics United States,
2008). The population of people with criminal convictions is growing at astronomical rates. This growth means
more and more Americans are legally barred from a large
portion of the gainful employment.

People with criminal convictions have variously been
barred from working in healthcare, childcare, education,
law enforcement, most (if not all) financial institutions,
justice, fire departments, the airline industry, the
armed forces. Former offenders are often barred from
professional licensure, i.e. lawyer, barber, or any field
requiring a liquor license.

Keep in mind that these sanctions are imposed
after people with a criminal conviction have paid their
debt to society. These sanctions have been proven to do
nothing other than contribute to the ongoing economic
depression of Blacks in this country. Furthermore, these
laws maintain white preference in hiring and destroy the
aspirations of Blacks and other minority groups. Blacks

have a difficult enough time gaining employment *without* a felony conviction (Pager, 2005). Why would a well-meaning politician adopt or support such draconian and malevolent penalties?

CHAPTER

4

WHAT ROLE DO CORRECTIONAL FACILITIES PLAY IN THE REHABILITATION PROCESS?

The NYSDOCS mission statement is "Enhance public safety by providing appropriate treatment services, in safe and secure facilities, that address the needs of all prisoners so they can return to their communities better prepared to lead successful and crime-free lives." No one would disagree with the goals of the New York State Department of Correctional Services, yet it appears that both executive and legislative branches of New York's state government have little confidence in the NYSDOCS achieving their mission.

How else could you explain such draconian penalties toward people with criminal convictions after they are released from NYSDOCS facilities? NYSDOCS has several programs that incarcerated people are required to complete to receive a "Certificate of Earned Eligibility." This certificate is a tool the department uses to highlight to the parole board that the incarcerated person successfully completed a rehabilitation program. The department assesses an incarcerated person's needs, and develops plans for rehabilitation. If you listen to the way the media and many politicians speak concerning people with criminal convictions, you would think that incarcerated people simply sit on their prison bunks for years and then come home at the end of their term. This is simply not true. In addition to the longer sentences people receive from the tough-on-crime laws passed in the nineties, the incarcerated receive services aimed at addressing the problems that may have contributed to their criminal behavior.

NYSDOCS has academic programs for prisoners who need to achieve their General Equivalency Diploma (GED). They also offer vocational training, substance abuse treatment, aggression replacement training, and sex offender counseling. Why are these programs funded if they do not count toward rehabilitation when the offenders return to their communities? This is a conflict of interest and a potential waste of tax dollars. Our government creates social problems so that some can profit from them. Upstate New York communities reap economic benefits from the booming prison industry. I recall a 1994 televised news story focused on a small upstate town. The residents were actually marching with signs calling for a prison to be placed in their county.

This mostly white town needed jobs desperately. They did not see any conflicts with their request for a *new* prison if it was to benefit their local economy—and the crimes that would have to be committed to fill the prison. After all, the prison-industrial complex is a business, and like all businesses, there is a need for a marketable product. A correctional facility's product is *people*.

New York State spends money on incarcerating citizens in upstate counties instead of adequately funding public schools or crime deterrence initiatives. I call this the *prison funding recycling system*. In this system, there is no fiscal conflict when it comes to funding mostly white communities. Our politicians, both liberal and conservative, do not consider it fiscally irresponsible to finance a failing correctional system as long as the beneficiaries of continued funding are primarily white citizens.

Most prison vocational programs and the actual skilled work learned by incarcerated people are worthless once the person is released. Incarcerated people that work throughout the state in various correctional facilities as clerks, janitors, and medical assistants are legally barred from returning to these positions once released. In addition, food service workers and library and teaching assistants are also legally barred from working in those fields after release. The time spent in the NYSDOCS programs thus has little value.

Under the prison funding recycling system, mostly white upstate communities reap the economic reward from the crime and punishment of mostly minority urban communities. The funding is funneled through a system of discrimination, racism, nepotism, and cronyism meant to maintain the dominance of whites as the main recipients of prosperity generated by criminal activity. The majority of NYSDOCS officers are white and disconnected socially and economically from the minority prisoner population. These officers are often hostile towards the imprisoned.

Tax dollars spent funding prisons in New York State equates to middle-class state jobs in post-industrial, economically challenged upstate communities, which means their tax dollars are spent back in their communities. This in turn boosts other businesses in their communities and creates more tax revenue for the state. Those tax dollars ultimately get funneled back to the NYSDOCS officers and staff, thus the prison funding recycling system. The racial problems in New York State are systemic. The number of incarcerated Black men in New York State amounts to an ethnic cleansing.

According to NYSDOCS statistics, out of 63,304 prisoners in 2006, 26,944 were new admissions. 62.6 percent of new admissions were new commitments (A person serving time on a new offense). There were 6,060 admitted for drug offenses, 4,878 for violent offenses, and 3,527 for property crimes. The average minimum sentence for violent offenders was 80.3 months. Nonviolent offenders averaged 26.1 months and youthful offenders 41.4 months. In 2006, out of the 6,060 admitted drug offenses, 59 percent were for drug sales and 41 percent were for drug possession. Males made up 93 percent of new commitments in 2006, and 96 percent of violent felony offenses.

Out of the 26,944 new admissions in 2006, 48.2 percent were Black, 26.5 percent were Hispanic or Latino, and 23.7 percent were white. Furthermore, out of 63,304 prisoners in NYSDOCS custody, 47.4 percent were from New York City, 12.2 percent were from suburban New York City, 20.9 percent were from upstate urban New

York, and 19.4 percent were from other areas of upstate New York.

All citizens need to discourage further discrimination within an already unrepresentative group. We cannot treat the sickness of discrimination with further discrimination. All of our citizens should be given a fair chance at employment opportunities.

In 1967, Martin Luther King, Jr. spoke eloquently of the effects of barring a person from a productive role in society:

> In our society it is murder psychologically to deprive a man of a job or an income. You are in substance saying to that man that he has no right to exist. You are in a real way depriving him of life, liberty and the pursuit of happiness, denying in his case the very creed of his society (King, 1967).

Every year, elected officials celebrate the birthday of Doctor King in our communities while at the same time turning a blind eye on the enormous, legally sanctioned discrimination against the formerly incarcerated all across New York State. The families of the formerly incarcerated are economically deprived as a result of the underemployment of their loved one.

A strong case can be made that public scrutiny of criminal records denies the families of the formerly convicted full rights to life, liberty and the pursuit of happiness under the law. Knowing that Blacks have the majority of criminal convictions in New York State, this civil rights infringement could be described as institutional racism. Social experts agree that the loss of a parent to prison, and the later lack of a financially productive parent, causes serious problems within the family unit. In the Black community, the rise in single-parent households has been a growing problem for the past twenty years. Those who would argue about the various problems single-parent homes cause are slow to make obvious connections between felony convictions, lack of employment and the dysfunctional households these two conditions spawn.

In order for NYSDOCS programs to work for the benefit and safety of our communities, civil death penalties must end after a set period of time. Their termination should be based on the rehabilitation efforts of the former offender.

NYSDOCS statistics show conclusively that prisoners who participate in their "Earned Eligibility Program," which offers targeted programs to fit individual needs, are less likely to offend again. In 2004, out of 14,681 releases, 69 percent remained out of NYSDOCS custody during a twenty-four-month period (NYSDOCS, 2007).

The state legislature's unwillingness to enact policies that actually cut crime is because of the hardships a smaller prison industry would cause to upstate rural (and mostly white) communities. A limit on the time civil death penalties against formerly convicted citizens would require employers to stop their widespread discrimination against this group.

The Princeton study showed that race alone often prevents Blacks from obtaining and maintaining gainful employment (Pager, 2005). Additionally, current statistics show that lack of post-prison employment leads to high recidivism rates. Many social scholars question the wisdom that employers actually have a legitimate interest in doing criminal background checks after a certain amount of time has passed from a former offender's release.

The policy of distrust of formerly convicted people *for life* is clearly a failed policy, judging by all of the statistics and empirical data over the past few years. Why is there so much resistance to true legislative change, reform that would actually stop punishing people long after they have paid their debt and desisted from committing criminal acts? Research proves conclusively that employers are not qualified or capable of making fair decisions regarding people with criminal backgrounds. An employer's need for criminal background information on potential employees decreases as time passes from the original offense and completed sentence.

The same claim of security interest, which an employer can reasonably make upon the initial release of a person with a criminal conviction, cannot be reasonably made after six to ten years of that person remaining free from criminal behavior and maintaining employment. The longer a person with a conviction remains free from criminal behavior, pays taxes, and maintains employment, the more unreasonable and irrelevant the request for criminal background information. At some point, a person's criminal record should be put behind them, for the greater good of society.

The greater good of society includes employers and even more importantly, the innocent children and families of the formerly incarcerated. Criminal behavior is present in every occupation from police departments to our state and federal governments. The Labor-Management

Reporting and Disclosure Act of 1959 (LMRDA) prohibits certain criminal offenders from holding specific positions in labor organizations for thirteen years (United States Department of Labor, 2007).

This law pertains to officials that commit crimes while holding office. Thirteen years is a long time, but at least there is an end to the prohibition eventually. If the LMRDA, a law that was meant to protect labor union members from corrupt, Mafia-connected union officials, offers a time limit in its punishment, civil death penalties could and should be limited as well. New York (along with most other states) prohibits people with criminal convictions from certain employment for life.

Since Blacks are arrested, convicted, and incarcerated at much higher rates than other groups, these civil death penalties disproportionately affect Black families. A good argument could be made that the impact of civil death penalties on the Black community is a violation of Title VII of the Civil Rights Act of 1964. This type of discrimination need not be intentional to be unlawful. The adverse impact that civil death penalties have on rehabilitated people with criminal convictions, spouses, children, extended family, and their communities is more important than the so-called reasonable interests of most employers.

At some point, formerly convicted people must be judged by their present condition. This is not possible under New York State's laws. The same impression most employers have of a person with a criminal conviction when they are first convicted or released from incarceration, is the same impression those employers will have after ten years of successful rehabilitation. The crime a person committed will never change, because there is no rewind in life, but the person can change. Each employer have personal opinions, prejudices, fears, and ignorance. Employers are not criminologists.

The system in effect in New York State strips away all confidence and dignity from formerly convicted people. People with criminal convictions are literally made to plead for mercy from employers every time they apply for a job. They must beg like dogs for low-level employment for *years* after the completion of their court-ordered punishment. These penalties are inhumane and should be done away with. The situation is particularly disturbing in light of the ongoing rise in undocumented immigrants, a group with no choice but to seek low-skill, low-paying jobs due to their status.

It has been estimated that there are now 12 to 20 million undocumented immigrants in the United States (United States Immigration Support, 2009). The estimated 16 million people (at least) with criminal convictions in the United States have problems finding jobs, and end up competing with undocumented immigrants for menial jobs. Civil death penalties are another disgraceful instance of racism and discrimination against Blacks and other minorities, an instance sanctioned and enacted by our government.

Many white employers appear to be sympathetic to other whites with criminal backgrounds (Pager and Western, 2005). This is a well-documented phenomenon and should not be discounted as hearsay. Many times we hear the media refer to white offenders as "misguided" or "disturbed," but Black criminals are described as "thugs," "hardened criminals," or "punks." Whites appear more willing to give a second chance to other whites with criminal convictions than to Blacks in the same situation.

CHAPTER

5

SHOULD CIVIL DEATH PENALTIES HAVE TIME LIMITS?

Civil death penalties should automatically end after ten years. These penalties affect more than just the offender. We need to seriously look at the ways these penalties negatively impact families. A financially unproductive father or mother naturally causes great stress on the family unit in an increasingly expensive capitalist society.

In New York City, the cost of living has gone up consistently each year. Housing, utilities, transportation, healthcare, and groceries cost a lot. The housing market has grown significantly, and in the last ten years, home prices in areas historically populated by minorities have doubled.

One study is pessimistic about the chances for low-income families in New York City: "Given the vastly higher cost of living in New York City, however, it is doubtful that any New York household that earns even $60,000 per year enjoys a quality of life that remotely approaches what we typically imagine as middle class" (Bowles, Kotkin and Giles, 2009).

A two-bedroom apartment that would have cost $800 a month in 1998 now rents for $1,600. Gainful employment is an absolute necessity. Low-wage jobs are the only option for most people with criminal convictions. The Princeton study found that the previously convicted tend to have a hard time obtaining even these less desirable jobs, with Blacks having the worst prospects. The unfortunate truth is that Article 23-A of the New York State Correction Law does not require that an employer make a conditional offer of employment to an applicant before requesting criminal background information, so there is no way to prove whether an employer has denied a person employment based specifically on their criminal background.

As a result of this, employers can easily avoid discrimination suits by simply denying the applicant for other reasons. If employers were required to make an initial offering of employment before criminal background data can be considered, a subsequently denied applicant would then know the employer has rejected him or her employment for criminal history reasons. The above oversight is one reason why charges are rarely filed pursuant to Article 23-A of the Correction Law.

The state of Hawaii and city of San Francisco require an initial offering of employment before most employers can request criminal background information. This is especially necessary when it pertains to public employment. New York employers still have the right to rely on criminal background in making their decision. This is a direct contradiction of Article 23-A of the Correction Law, which is intended to prohibit unfair discrimination against persons previously convicted of one or more criminal offenses. Certificates of good conduct only create the presumption of rehabilitation. Article 23-A is an *ineffective* attempt to solve a very complex problem. Civil death penalties have kept recidivism rates high in the New York State criminal justice system for decades. Most people would agree that single-parent households negatively affect the children in the household. An unemployed parent even—more affects a family (economically) than an absent parent. Employers have a legitimate interest in knowing about the criminal backgrounds of formerly convicted applicants when they are first released. However, a formerly convicted person's children, spouse, and community have an even greater interest in seeing them become productively employed citizens.

"If indeed there are serious rehabilitative efforts undertaken by a person while serving time in prison, what good is it if no opportunities are apparent for him or her once they are released?" (Boothe, 2007)

This is why time limits should be placed on civil death penalties. In doing so, the *legitimate* interests of the entire community would be protected. Employers should not be allowed to deny employment to people with criminal convictions long after they have been rehabilitated. This oversight has caused a disaster in the Black community. The correlation between the extremely high conviction rates and unemployment rates for Blacks in New York State should raise a red flag for lawmakers.

For legislators not to acknowledge this correlation is equivalent to walking in the rain without an umbrella and questioning why you are getting wet.

CHAPTER

6

HOW DO CIVIL DEATH PENALTIES AFFECT BLACKS ECONOMICALLY?

In 2006, out of a population of 19,306,183 residents of New York State, 17.4 percent were African-American, 60.5 percent were white, and 16.3 percent were of Latino origin. In 2002, out of 1,707,168 firms owned in the state, only 7.6 percent were Black-owned (United States Census Bureau, 2006).

These numbers are especially relevant in my argument, considering the longstanding history of white domination over the economic condition of Blacks. "The value of Black labor has always been controlled by the white community" (Anderson, 1994).

A majority of the white population does not mind sharing the economic prosperity of our state and country. However, in order for a large percentage of Blacks to share equally in prosperity, some whites may have to share in poverty. There are simply not enough good jobs to accommodate everyone.

"Capitalistic democracies have historically accepted a certain level of unemployment as a necessary public good and permitted businesses to use unemployment as a device for maintaining low wages" (Anderson, 1994). Unfortunately, Blacks have had to bear the burden of unemployment in our white-dominated society. Our economy is faltering and the world's resources are growing scarce. Therefore, we may soon have to not only compete for employment, but for food and shelter as well. As the American dollar loses value around the world, we may find it harder to maintain the traditional American standard of living. Blacks have been able to get by and often flourish without the many amenities most whites are accustomed to having.

Violence pervades the Black community. Daily we are bombarded with the grim realities of living in a world of racial inequality. Ethnic identity is a very important aspect of our lives. Yet how can a child envision a positive future when they do not see positive role models around them?

Blacks have had to cope with ethnic cleansing in the form of the banishment of our males from society. Not only does incarceration reduce the population of available males for reproduction, it also adds to the number of single-parent households. Employers should not be allowed to scrutinize and use criminal background information against (rehabilitated) formerly convicted people. Employment discrimination disparately impact even Blacks with no criminal background.

There is a sense of hopelessness in the Black community. This hopelessness has caused an emergence of degenerate behavioral patterns. These behavioral patterns have replaced traditional Black culture. We now see an emerging thug culture. The gangster image is the order of the day, and threatens to taint Black men and women for years to come. Comedian Dave Chappelle said it best in 2000: "Why wear a whore uniform if you are not a whore?" (Lathan, 2000) If you are not a gangster, rap star, or thug, why dress like one? A popular dress style for urban youth consists of a du-rag on their head, a jacket with a hood, earrings, pants hanging below their buttocks exposing their underwear; and dark clothing to further solidify a bad-guy image. Yet many of these youth are not dangerous at all. They are only emulating a popular behavior and dress style. This is prison culture spilling over into free society. In prison, prisoners have to project an image of strength. They must live on the defensive, every day.

They must also show that they are not targets for everyday features of prison life like rape, robbery, and assault. Still, a good number of these men are not dangerous at all. Still, this gangster style of clothing has lasted for over a decade. In the past, fads typically lasted for a year or so, and did not project a dangerous image. In the eighties, Bally and Clarks shoes were popular. The popular style of dress then involved a fresh, groomed look. This was reinforced by rap groups like the Get Fresh Crew and rappers like Slick Rick and Doug E. Fresh.

Other rap performers, including Eric B and Rakim, Run DMC and LL Cool J, had a positive message in their music. In the nineties, the message of hip-hop transformed into one of (mostly) misogyny and hedonism. Womanizing and violence began to dominate the lyrics of rappers. The removal of the male from the typical Black household is an old strategy used by the power elite to weaken the Black family structure. This method of divide and conquer was first utilized on Blacks by slave owners.

Historically, separating the sexes has been used to maintain low achievement levels in Blacks. Black women are forced to be both mother and father to their children. Formerly convicted Blacks face enormous obstacles in obtaining and retaining employment, and this affects the Black family unit.

"By knowing the nature, circumstances, and slave making methods that laid the basis for Black male and female relationships during the slave trade, Black America as a collective begins to up-root the foundation of our division" (Morrow, 2003).

Our government must reevaluate existing legislation to determine if it has achieved its intended goals. Title VII of the Civil Rights Act of 1964 was intended to prevent discriminatory practices. Title VII should be strengthened, particularly its clauses on disparate treatment and disparate impact. This clause, if clarified, could offer relief from the civil death penalties visited upon formerly convicted people.

Blacks represent a minority of drug users in this country, yet receive the majority of mandatory drug sentences and the civil death penalties that follow. Blacks are prosecuted and convicted of crimes more often than whites arrested for similar crimes. Current criminal justice statistics point to a blatant form of discrimination.

Civil death penalties should be amended to reflect the primary goal of correctional facilities: to rehabilitate prisoners. Some Non Profit Organizations that advocate for formerly convicted people are not willing to push for legislative change to civil death penalties because they fear the loss of their core clientele which are formerly convicted people.

Nonprofit organizations often support legislation that maintains the status quo, and allows them to continue receiving funding for services that are generally ineffective in helping formerly convicted people obtain gainful employment. Job search preparation and training are necessary skills that people with criminal convictions need to obtain employment. The Princeton study used testers who were well-spoken, well-dressed and attractive to the eyes. Yet their race and (fictional) criminal backgrounds outweighed any positives. There is also a lack of funding for addressing psychological issues in people who have served considerable time in prison.

Incarceration in some ways is similar to being a soldier in a war zone. This is not meant to detract from the great sacrifices our veterans have made to advance the causes of democracy and freedom. In many ways, atrocities experienced by soldiers on the battlefield are also experienced in correctional facilities across the nation. Murder, rape, and assault are all daily events in prisons. However, soldiers get paid for their services and are able to go home every now and then to get a reprieve from the violence. If soldiers suffer from post-traumatic stress disorder after exposure to such things on a temporary basis, imagine the damage inflicted upon a prisoner exposed to the same violence for years on end.

The prisoner is then released into society with a bus ticket and $40 in hand and civil death penalties hanging over his or her head. The psychological stress of imprisonment may be one reason why formerly incarcerated people are often introverted and "institutionalized" to the point that they find it impossible to maintain a law-abiding lifestyle. Many formerly incarcerated people suffer from post traumatic stress disorder and do not receive mental health services.

Formerly convicted people should be given a real opportunity to redeem themselves. However, they must first clearly demonstrate that they have been employed, obeyed the law, paid taxes, and addressed the problems that lead to their criminal behavior. Civil death penalty laws may have to be removed judicially and not legislatively. Many politicians tend to shy away from amending these laws for fear of being branded "soft on crime."

Limiting the employment opportunities of people with criminal convictions after they have paid their debt to society is cruel and unusual punishment. Since no human being in our society can survive without food and shelter, our government should never put up obstacles for formerly convicted people in providing food and shelter for themselves and their families.

The 2006 Kurlychek et al study found that formerly convicted people, after seven years (after release or conviction); do not commit crimes at rates much higher than non-offenders. The argument often made by employers that they will face negligent hiring lawsuits for hiring formerly convicted people in New York State is outdated due to recent legislation. However, it should be noted that an employer will be no less liable for criminal acts by an employee without an existing criminal background. There are simple ways to protect employers from liability. Sealing criminal records of all proven rehabilitated former offenders after a period of time could also be good for the economy due to increased tax revenue by formerly convicted people who would otherwise be unemployed and indigent.

Another recent bill (#A05330) sponsored by Assemblyman Aubry "establishes it shall be an unlawful discriminatory practice for any prospective employer to make an inquiry about, or to act upon adversely to the individual involved based upon, any criminal conviction of such individual unless such employer first makes a conditional offer of employment to such individual." Regarding the fiscal implications of the bill Aubry writes: "Successful re-entry and re-integration of formerly incarcerated individuals will increase state revenues through the inclusion of thousands of able-bodied, 'taxpaying' citizens to the state's workforce; additional savings to the state will inure from a reduction in costs associated with recidivism, re-incarceration and social services" (Aubry, 2009).

Section 1, subdivision 15 of section 296 of the executive law (which was signed into law by Governor David Paterson on September 4, 2008) relieves employers from negligent hiring suits by allowing them a "rebuttable presumption" to exclude from evidence a person's background information. This law pertains to employers that follow the guidelines of Article 23-A of the Correction Law (Aubry and Volker, 2008).

A person with a certificate of good conduct or certificate of relief from disabilities shields employers against negligent hiring lawsuits. Most people with criminal convictions can be fully rehabilitated. The rehabilitation process starts in correctional facilities. Many of our elected officials dismiss outright the programs that incarcerated people attend in correctional facilities. The significant time prisoners spend in correctional facilities cannot be discounted in evaluating rehabilitation. Parole boards base their decisions in part on a prisoner's program participation.

Denying a prisoner parole based on the seriousness of their offense is a common practice. Incarcerated people have several benchmarks to meet before they can make it home. Furthermore, if they *are* released on parole, the parole board sets conditions that must be followed in their release papers. One of these conditions is to obtain and maintain employment. Many criminal offenders have or have had alcohol and drug dependency problems that may have contributed to their criminal activity. As a result, they are required to attend treatment programs upon release. New York is spending billions of dollars on rehabilitative programs known as "targeted programs."

Mayor Ray Nagin of New Orleans made this statement at Tavis Smiley's "State of The Black Union" event in 2008: "We have to reclaim our prison population, second chance, and third chance, whatever it takes." Drugs and violence go hand in hand. It should be no surprise that the crack epidemic brought a rise in violent crime. If we are going to have a serious conversation about discrimination against formerly convicted people, we should not start that conversation by discriminating against certain offenders.

CHAPTER

7

DISCRIMINATORY PRACTICES IN HIRING PEOPLE WITH CRIMINAL CONVICTIONS

White-owned businesses have historically discriminated against Blacks in this country. Dividing Blacks by nationality, gender, conviction status and age has always been the standard in maintaining the dominant position of whites. The practice of divide-and-conquer has maintained white privilege. Rare examples of Blacks in power include former Secretaries of State Colin Powell and Condoleezza Rice. Most Blacks in high positions must assimilate the dominant white culture. Additionally, Black males have been further discriminated against by employers who give preference to Black women in hiring. This is especially true in office jobs, or positions that require meaningful public interaction. Black woman are believed to be less threatening.

"America has maintained a racial and ethnic ranking of preference" (Anderson, 1994). Latinos have become the preferred group to hire. The rationale given by employers is that Latinos have a good work ethic. The truth is that employers want to exploit undocumented immigrants. This is not to say Latinos do not work hard.

Many politicians want to pass legislation allowing the estimated 12 to 20 million undocumented immigrants to obtain citizenship, while at the same time placing insurmountable obstacles in the way of the roughly 16 million people with criminal convictions. This is another testament to the malevolent lack of concern for the aspirations of people with criminal convictions and their families in this country.

There is a growing sentiment around the country that most criminal records should automatically be sealed from public scrutiny after a period of time has passed from the end of a sentence or release date. "There should be a full-scale discussion of the criminal justice system and automatic pardons for most people with criminal convictions after they pay their debts to society" (Maddox, 2008).

Americans have been living under some of the uncivilized and archaic customs of ancient Europe. People with criminal convictions are used to fuel the prison-industrial complex and supply clients to nonprofits, who also live off the decaying carcasses former offenders often become when faced with civil death penalties.

Rehabilitating formerly convicted people reduces crime and recidivism. Ideological politicians have the tendency to demonize violent offenders as unredeemable, unworthy of a second chance via expunged records or spent sentences. This demonization of one group is just the kind of mindless inconsideration of all of the factors of criminal behavior (When a sentence becomes spent, the conviction(s) the sentence covers cannot be used against you in employment, housing or licensure).

Must there be a permanent underclass? Most people with criminal convictions did not cause permanent damage to society. Criminal offenders who commit murder, considered to be the most violent crime, have the lowest rate of recidivism.

Many recent studies about discrimination against those with criminal convictions when seeking employment show the same basic truth: people with criminal convictions are often denied employment for a past offense long after they have been rehabilitated from the offense.

CHAPTER

8

SHOULD COURTS INFORM CRIMINAL DEFENDANTS ABOUT CIVIL DEATH PENALTIES?

A large percentage of criminal defendants in America would not plead guilty if they knew about the civil death penalties awaiting them after completion of their sentence. There would be less incentive for criminal defendants to plea-bargain. New York State allows the civil confinement of sexual offenders after they have completed their sentence. New York University law professor Steven Schulhofer, who specialized in criminal procedures, states:

> I think it's very powerful speculation that this kind of bill would take away most of the incentive for anyone to plead guilty because they would be facing the prospect for indefinite confinement potentially for the rest of their lives. It would

force defendants to go to trial (Gershman, 2006).

Perhaps if judges were required to explain to criminal defendants the civil death penalties they will face after serving their sentence, more defendants would go to trial and ultimately overburden the system. This would discourage relying on simple incarceration as a means of addressing crime. In most cases minority defendants cannot afford the bail set. Instead, they are forced to linger in detention centers such as Rikers Island, located in the New York City borough of Queens. Some detainees remain on Rikers Island for years before their cases are resolved. Rikers Island is well-known to be one of the worst places to be detained in New York. The living conditions are reported by former detainees to be dismal. Detainees are often crowded into dormitories with poor ventilation. Violence is inescapable for detainees on Rikers Island. An information campaign should be waged in our homes, schools, colleges, and universities to inform citizens about the civil death penalties facing former offenders.

Every effort must be made to bring attention to the massive discrimination formerly convicted people face after their sentences are complete. Civil death penalties disproportionately affect the Black community. Those who claim that civil death penalties are not a direct punishment from a felony conviction are simply wrong. Most employers will deny employment to people with criminal convictions. Police officers are statutorily required to read a suspect the Miranda warnings when making an arrest. Why are Miranda rights so important? Miranda rights are necessary to inform the person being arrested of their right to remain silent, and their right to an attorney either hired or appointed by the courts.

The key phrase in the Miranda warning is "Anything you say can be used against you in a court of law." This statement implies that there can be legal consequences for any information divulged by arrestees. This same reasoning should be added to Article 23-A of the corrections law. There is civil death consequences applied to every criminal sentence. This would help in generating broader awareness of civil death penalties, which would ultimately be part of a fairer approach to crime and punishment.

Offenders should know the consequences of accepting a plea bargain for what they may believe is a shorter sentence. These plea bargains do not mention the fact that civil death penalties of that plea will last a lifetime. If the civil death penalties of criminal convictions were widely understood by the public, perhaps fewer people would commit crimes.

CHAPTER

9

SHOULD A CRIMINAL CONVICTION BE CONSIDERED A DISABILITY?

The 2003 US-led invasion ravaged Iraq. The war's collateral damage necessitated the assistance of the United States in rebuilding the country. This is the very same logic that should be used to bring legislative change to civil death penalties. Civil death penalties are not directly connected to convictions. Courts impose sentences, not collateral penalties such as civil death penalties. Civil Death Penalties are a part of the legislative process. Thus the offender is not actually at fault for the penalties imposed after they serve out the term of their sentence. If people with criminal convictions were to file a civil lawsuit alleging that they should not have to suffer civil death penalties due to the fact that they were not informed at the time of sentencing, the courts would probably rule that these consequences are not directly related to the plaintiffs' convictions.

Offenders can be effectively punished without tacking on civil death penalties. These laws are simply dinosaurs that should be extinct. Dozens of reports and books by elite thinkers and advocates suggest that formerly convicted people should be given a real second chance. However, some advocates posit that only nonviolent offenders should receive a second chance. These penalties are causing financial disabilities to formerly convicted people and should be subsidized by Social Security-style benefits.

Supplementary income benefits should be paid to people with criminal convictions until the laws are changed. People with criminal convictions pay taxes like everyone else, even violent offenders and sex offenders. Yet formerly convicted people are inarguably discriminated against. Formerly convicted people are the lepers of our day. Why does society have the right to shun formerly incarcerated people after they have paid their debt? A debt is something that can be paid in full.

If a person is willing (if not *forced*) to pay the debt in full, why is any sanction needed or allowed? Forgiveness is a bedrock Judeo-Christian principle, yet it is a hard sell to individuals with motives at odds with doctrines of redemption. The prison-industrial complex is operated by people who plan to keep their business profitable.

This can only be achieved by creating specific social and economic situations that spawn criminal behavior and recidivism. It is no coincidence that Blacks often reside in failing school districts. Many advocates believe there is a "school to prison pipeline." For the most part, drug offenders are understood to be nonviolent by advocates of civil death penalty reform. Yet there are victims in drug trafficking. Illegal drugs give rise to other offenses, both violent and nonviolent in nature.

It is not fair to give second chances to only nonviolent offenders. Any offender who demonstrates rehabilitation should be given a second chance at life, liberty, and the pursuit of happiness. We need to give them the opportunity to put their past behind them. A good model for New York State to follow is Canada's pardons policy. In a study titled "Setting Aside Criminal Convictions in Canada: A Successful Approach to Offender Reintegration," it was stated:

> Expunging a criminal conviction in the United States is a rare event and often limited to persons who committed offenses as juveniles or adult misdemeanants. Criminal convictions in Canada, however, are routinely set aside through pardons after offenders have demonstrated a period of crime-free behavior … Although setting aside criminal convictions seems inconsistent with the increasing use of collateral consequences for U.S. offenders, taking this approach might contribute to increased public safety in the long term by easing offender reintegration … The fact that almost 97 percent of Canadian offenders who were pardoned are successful attests to their effectiveness; some have now remained without further conviction for more than three decades. This is a strong argument for pursuing similar strategies beyond the borders of Canada.

> Although such approaches may not be po-
> litically popular within the United States,
> they embody characteristically American
> values; giving individuals an opportunity
> to redeem themselves, rewarding law-
> abiding behavior, and giving somebody
> who has made a mistake a second chance
> (Ruddell and Winfree, 2006).

We must not allow a large percent of our citizens to be shut out of a second chance. If the rationale for second-chance legislation is to make nonviolent offenders employable, then it is totally irresponsible to suggest that the offenders having the hardest time finding employment should *never* be given a second chance. Many studies show that unemployment is a prelude to criminal activity. Allowing employers to use outdated and irrelevant criminal convictions to deny applicants employment is exacerbating the crime problem in New York State.

The burden of crime is placed on our communities. The burden of punishment is placed on the criminal offender. The burden of issuing punishment is placed on the criminal justice system. However, the legislative bodies that pass draconian laws are not burdened at all. The New York State Senate is one such body that regularly passes tough-on-crime legislation. Though the majority of criminal activity affects the cities of New York, rural Republicans in the New York State Senate dictate legislative agendas in Albany.

New York City and other urban majority-minority populations are at the mercy of racially divisive politicians that are totally cut off from the crime problem. These politicians are destroying families in community districts that they do not represent. Because of partisan politics, detachment, and racism, these politicians turn a blind eye to the plight of other communities. New York State should be the very first employer of people with criminal convictions. The laws that place civil death penalties on people with criminal convictions in New York State are the products of these legislators. The New York legislature has to take responsibility for their actions. If the effects of civil death penalties on the Black community are despair, high unemployment, broken families, and crime, the state that implemented the policy has a moral and ethical responsibility to support those it has disabled. If civil death penalties did not exist, people with criminal convictions could put their past behind them and move forward in pursuit of happiness.

Employment would be more easily attainable. Employers have several methods for denying employment to people with criminal convictions. Employers do not have to see you before they deny you employment. Increasingly, employers ask applicants to mail in their resumes. Most employers have accounts with Internet-based background check sites. These sites charge under $20 for background checks, and often give discounts to companies who bring repeat business. Employers can basically deny employment to people with criminal convictions by claiming they hired a more experienced candidate.

In New York State, there are no laws that adequately protect people with criminal convictions from unfair discrimination. The New York State Division of Human Rights law provides that employers and licensing agencies have to consider the following in regards to people with criminal convictions:

1. New York's public policy to encourage licensure and employment of those with previous convictions.

2. The specific duties and responsibilities necessarily related to the license or employment sought.

3. The bearing, if any, the criminal offense for which the person was previously convicted will have on his/her fitness or ability to perform such duties or responsibilities.

4. The time that has elapsed since the occurrence of the criminal offense.

5. The age of the person at the time of the occurrence of the criminal offense.

6. The seriousness of the criminal offense.

7. Any information produced by the person, or produced on his/her behalf; in regard to his/her rehabilitation and good conduct (New York State Division of Human Rights, 2009).

There are no laws preventing employers from denying employment to an applicant with a criminal conviction. Article 23-A does not adequately protect people with criminal convictions from unfair discrimination. Not only do people with criminal convictions have to file an Article 78 civil charge, which is not free and could take months or even years to complete, former offenders must request that an employer send them notice, in writing, about their decision and how NYSDHR factors were applied in making that decision.

It is also important to realize that employers do not have unlimited job openings. Most of the time, employers advertise for only a few positions, if they advertise them at all. A growing trend is word-of-mouth hiring's, also known as networking. Ethnic groups often refer people of their own background and origin to jobs at their place of work. It is not uncommon to find one ethnic group dominating the employment rolls at New York hospitals, restaurants, or hotels. This is not a coincidence.

New York, as a state, is one of the worst violators of the human rights of people with criminal convictions. Every time well-intentioned legislation is proposed to alleviate this crisis, the media, legislators, and employers reject it.

Our country is headed toward hard economic times. If we do not begin to practice forgiveness and believe in rehabilitation, we might see desperate actions by millions of people with criminal convictions, forced to resort to any available means to support themselves and their families.

Employers simply cannot have it both ways. If employers will not agree on spent sentences for (rehabilitated) formerly convicted people, then employers should have to pay extra taxes to underwrite public benefits for these people. People with criminal convictions will need to prove that they are truly rehabilitated by some sort of certification process, such as the process described in Article 23-A of the Correction Law.

It is unjust and uncivilized for New York State to allow employers to use criminal backgrounds to deny employment to people with criminal convictions. When a person is first released from prison, it is reasonable for an employer to be unsure regarding a potential relapse. However, based on empirical data, after a decade of desistance it becomes unreasonable for an employer to use criminal conviction status to measure the suitability of a job applicant.

It is in the best interest of the community for those with criminal convictions to find and keep gainful employment. Employers are only one side of this conversation, yet they have been able to dictate the agenda completely. They have discouraged lawmakers from passing meaningful legislation that could actually reduce crime. There are many legislators, correction officers, and law enforcement officials who desire things to stay just as they are. These parties profit from crime while the community suffers. New York has created an employment disability for people with criminal convictions.

In a recent report by the New York Civil Liberties Union titled "The Marijuana Arrest Crusade in New York City: Racial Bias in Police Policy 1997-2007," it was found that "the NYPD arrested and jailed nearly 400,000 people for possessing small amounts of marijuana between 1997 and 2007, a tenfold increase in marijuana arrests over the previous decade and a figure marked by startling racial and gender disparities." The report highlighted those disparities: "between the years 1997 and 2007, 205,000 Blacks, 122,000 Latinos and 59,000 whites were jailed for low level marijuana offenses. Blacks only represented 26 percent of the city's population, while representing 52 percent of the arrested. Latinos represented 27 percent of the city's population, while representing 31 percent of the arrested. Whites represented 35 percent of the population while only representing 15 percent of those arrested for marijuana offenses" (Levine and Small, 2008). This shows racial profiling on a large scale. This alone is cause to push for change to existing state laws that permanently restrict employment opportunities from people with criminal convictions.

If a person commits a crime, that person should pay the price. The punishment should, at all times, fit the crime. Nonviolent offenders should not be treated as harshly as violent offenders. However, we are not talking about fair punishment when we refer to civil death penalties. We are talking about lifetime restrictions placed on people by the state *after* their punishment has been completed. Civil death penalties are insidious and inhumane. Social Security disability benefits should be paid to people with criminal convictions until they are no longer denied equal and fair rights to obtain employment. The stigma of a criminal conviction is dreadful enough to potentially keep a person unemployed or underemployed for life. Politicians have openly admitted as much—and have recently sponsored legislation to seal the public records of criminal offenders with drug-related crimes so they can avoid discrimination when searching for employment.

Studies prove without a doubt that most employers will not knowingly hire a person with a criminal record. These same studies show that white employers give preference to white applicants over Black—even if the white jobseeker has a criminal conviction and the Black applicant has no criminal history (Pager and Western,

2003). If employers had to pay extra taxes to finance benefits to the people they refuse to employ, they would soon realize it would be in their best interest to support limits on civil death penalties.

CHAPTER

10

HAS ARTICLE 23-A OF THE CORRECTION LAW BEEN SUCCESSFUL?

Bills S-4222-C and A-5393-C were joint efforts of the New York State Senate and Assembly during their respective 1975-1976 regular sessions. These bills lead to the provisions in Article 23-A of the New York State Corrections Law which was an attempt to protect people with criminal convictions from unfair discrimination in employment and licensure. The bills were introduced by State Senators Paterson Sr., Marino, Goodman, Gold, Garcia, and Galiber, and Assemblymen Fink and Reilly. Article 23-A of the Correction Law authorizes the issuance of certificates of relief from disability and certificates of good conduct to formerly convicted people. That article also sets guidelines for employers and licensing agencies to follow when considering the employment or licensing of people with criminal convictions. These bills, which amended both the Correction Law and the Executive

Law in relation to the removal of disabilities of criminal offenders and repealing other provisions, are the finished versions of legislation debated in 1975.

Bill S-4222-C was an extremely weakened version of the much stronger Bill S-5393-C. New York legislators have a history of caving into the unreasonable paranoia and fears of partisan politicians and racially divisive employers, who discriminate against Blacks with or without convictions. Bill S-5393-C, introduced by Assemblyman Fink, put a time limit on criminal background information requests. Fink had provisions in his bill that restricted civil death penalties that accompany a criminal conviction. At the time, Fink wrote:

> Employers, unions and other organizations seeking employment information would be prohibited from inquiring of an applicant for any licensing or economic right or employment opportunity as to (1) whether the applicant has a record of arrest, (2) whether the applicant has been convicted of a felony, or released from actual confinement, other than within the past seven years, or (3) whether the applicant has been convicted of a misdemeanor, or released from actual confinement, other than within the past three years (Fink, 1976).

The State of Hawaii has a law similar to Fink's original bill. Hawaii has very low crime and recidivism rates.

What happened to Assemblyman Fink's bill is unknown. However, a compromise was reached.

Assemblyman Fink wrote in a memorandum in support of Senator Marino's bill that:

> Unemployment is the greatest deterrence to rehabilitation as statistics indicate that many of the people with criminal convictions return to lives of crime because other employment is not available ... [this bill] would lift job restrictions from rehabilitated people with criminal convictions now deprived of over 125 licensing and employment categories because of their criminal records (Fink, 1976).

Then-governor Hugh L. Carey eventually approved Marino's Bill S-4222-C. But before he signed the bill, he gave employers and both state and local government agencies an opportunity to approve or disapprove of the proposed amendments. Below are some of the letters sent to Carey regarding S-4222-C:

LETTERS IN FAVOR

New York State Coalition for Criminal Justice Policy Committee Chairperson I. Jackson, head of a coalition of sixty non-profit and advocacy groups, wrote on May 8, 1975: "The Coalition, in a letter sent to all members of the Assembly, called the eleven bill package an *acceptable baseline* for correctional reform ... People with criminal convictions are discouraged from seeking lawful employment by endless discriminatory barriers encountered in public and pri-vate employment. We support a bill to repeal outdated barriers, bar unjustified discrimination and pro-vide a logical procedure for discretionary relief from remaining disabilities."

B. Rowan of the New York State Bar Association wrote on July 7, 1976: "The Civil Rights Committee is delighted to comment favorably on this proposed Act … We proposed a similar but some-what less comprehensive scheme in 1975, and again in 1976, with no success. While some members of the committee may feel that more aggressive legislation is required, the general consensus is that this step is long overdue and quite appropriate in the present punitive political atmosphere."

American Bar Association Commis-sioner R. McKay wrote on July 7, 1976: "We are pleased to learn that S-4222-C, a bill designed to relieve discriminatory employment practices against people with criminal convictions, has passed the New York Legislature. We respectfully urge you to sign this important measure into law."

New York State Executive Department Division of Human Rights Commis-sioner W. Kramarsky wrote on July

12, 1976: "The proposed Section 755 of the Correction Law treats cases involving public agencies differently from cases involving private employers, while the proposed Section 296.15 of the Human Rights Law makes no such distinction ... Despite these defects, the bill is a commendable effort to deal with the employment problems of people with criminal convictions, and the State Division of Human Rights recommends that the Governor approve the bill."

New York State Department of Labor Commissioner P. Ross wrote on July 15, 1976: "The bill has the desirable purpose of aiding in the rehabilitation of former convicts."

New York Civil Liberties Union Legislative Director B. Shack wrote on July 9, 1976: "Automatic prohibitions and reflexive limitations pertaining to the employment of ex-offenders are arbitrary, irrational and dysfunctional ... They only serve to increase the frustration and desperation of such persons and to encourage their return to crime ... To the extent that this bill would help remove these employment barriers, it is long over-due and should be enacted."

Citizens Union of the City of New York Associate Director S. Shestokofsky

wrote on April 12, 1976: "This bill would provide a comprehensive approach to broadening employment opportunities for people with criminal convictions ... It would automatically bar arbitrary discrimination against rehabilitated people with criminal convictions seeking licensure, public or private employment, by forbidding bias based on 'stale' convictions (felonies older than 7 years and misdemeanors older than 3 years of the date of release from actual confinement being the triggering mechanism for the statute)."

LETTERS OPPOSED

Colt Industries Vice President of employee relations T. Ward Jr. wrote on July 23, 1976: "The provisions in this proposed legislation, which are particularly disturbing, deal with the additional unreasonable restrictions it would place on the employers of New York State in the area of personnel selection. ... In fact, it is reaching a point where, in some cases, the employer is hardly permitted the opportunity to make the best choice in the selection of its personnel, but the choice that must satisfy one or more, if not all, of these agencies."

Lipe-Rollway Corporations Corporate Director of Industrial Relations E. Smith wrote on July 23, 1976: "The net result of this legislation as amended would be to subject the employer to excessive harassment and ultimate financial burden."

Gray-Syracuse Inc. Chairman R. Gray wrote on July 22, 1976: "As a small businessman, I am surprised to learn about the contents of the above bill to make it illegal to deny employment to persons previously convicted of even serious criminal offenses."

Vega Industries Executive Vice President D. Jaquith wrote on July 22, 1976: "This is a bad bill for business. It attempts to legislate employment standards in the private sector, and my company is strongly opposed to it. It imposes personnel hiring practices that can adversely affect the quality of our work force."

Facet Enterprises Inc. Director of Industrial Relations R. Snowden wrote on July 16, 1976: "The nature of accepting or rejecting applicants for employment is such that it might not relate in any way to past criminal offenses, yet a convicted person would naturally believe such to be the case and be hard to convince otherwise."

Church & Dwight Co. Personnel Manager B. Wittlin wrote on July 21, 1976: "If I understand rationale correctly, a past offender has paid his debt to society and, therefore, should not be further discriminated against. If this is the case, I could not agree more wholeheartedly with the intent. My concern, however, is that this legislation pre-supposes that all past offenders have been sufficiently and adequately rehabilitated to be useful to public citizens once again."

The Graser Co. President R. Bevard wrote on July 20, 1976: "It is inconceivable to me, and to several other businessmen with whom I have regular contact, how the legislature and/or the Executive Branch of the State government can continue to burden business with these non-productive activities … This particular bill and its amendments not only are contrary to the best interest of the business community, but also the labor community … It impinges upon the dignity in general of the labor component of our economy and specifically upon those who would be effected by it."

These are only a few of the arguments that will be made when our leaders in government again take up the cause of reasonable second-chance legislation. These statements reveal the methods employers use to avoid hiring people with criminal convictions. Avoiding addressing a person's criminal past but ultimately denying that person employment gets employers off the hook. In fact, employers in New York State never have to hire a person with a criminal conviction. Employers do not even have to consider the full scope of Article 23-A. A hiring company can simply say "After careful consideration of your application, we decided to choose another candidate."

The Commission on Human Rights held public hearings in May 1972 at the New York University Law Center. These hearings focused on the employment problems people with criminal convictions were having at that time. The chair of the hearings was Eleanor Holmes Norton. In her opening remarks, she said this:

> Blatant job discrimination against people with criminal convictions makes prison an employment of last resort for many who return there … Yet discrimination against people with criminal convictions seems to many a contradiction in terms … If a person has been judged guilty of a crime, how can we expect that they will perform on a job like the rest of us? … Rather than take a chance, why not simply bar people with criminal convictions from most jobs and protect ourselves? … We have protected ourselves least with this philosophy … We will never know just how many men and women have been

literally driven back into crime by the no-work rules we impose on people with criminal convictions ... But this we do know: Prison in America is the kind of experience that makes most who come out want to do whatever they can to avoid going back ... Society starts working against its own interest while men and women are still in prison ... The incarcerated are shorn of every personal dignity and liberty, and then tossed out un-rehabilitated and un-supported to reintegrate into a society that is increasingly as hostile to them as it is anxious about the crime that many are driven to by joblessness ... This heartless and mindless exclusion from jobs has especially tragic effects on Blacks and Puerto Ricans, who go to prison in disproportionate numbers ... Poorly educated and discriminated against while law-abiding, they become pariahs once they get a record. David Rothenberg of the Fortune Society says that a white person with criminal convictions has two strikes against him, but a Black released from prison is out of the ball game ... Over the past several years, the country has come to recognize that racial discrimination now infects American life in strange new ways ... Entire institutions have become enclaves of the poor,

Brown, and Black. Nowhere is this more ominous than in prisons ... To be sure, prisons have always been repositories for society's underclass ... But because of the peculiarities of the American experience, a dangerous link between race and prison has been forged ... Prisons dominated by young Black and brown men symbolize the society's most awesome failure (City of New York Commission on Human Rights, 1972).

If you did not know that these hearings were held in 1972, you might think that Ms. Norton had made her statement just yesterday. Her words here were spoken thirty-seven years ago. Even given the protections of Article 23-A, nothing has changed in New York State since her remarks. We have the same rules, only different players trying to advocate for formerly convicted people in New York State. Below are some of the findings and recommendations of the 1972 commission:

STATE AND CITY LEGISLATION

- "To prohibit denial of licenses solely on the basis of a prior criminal record and restricting denials to those instances where there is either a clear relation of a prior offense to the license (or job) sought and insufficient evidence of rehabilitation."

- "To amend New York State Civil Service Law so that it enunciates a positive policy toward people with criminal convictions, limits exclusion to job-related offenses and instances of insufficient rehabilitation, provides review procedures and requires an annual statistical summary of people with criminal convictions applications and actions."

- "To amend Human Rights Laws to include people with criminal convictions as a protected class, restricting questions that may be asked or information acted on by employers."

- "To amend statutes governing issuance of Certificates of Relief from Disabilities and of Good Conduct to provide automatic issuance, a shorter waiting period and mandatory acceptance by licensing authorities and public employers."

FEDERAL LEGISLATION

- "To provide close control over arrest and conviction data [and its] dissemination and place a time limit on the availability of criminal records."

PROGRAM REFORM

- "Re-design of prison work experience, education and training to develop a coordinated system throughout city and state facilities, emphasizing work and educational release, with all vocational rehabilitation directed toward current New York City labor market trends."

- "Establish a job analysis and development capacity within the correctional system."

- "Develop close working relations between the correctional system and business and labor to assure relevance of training and secure commitments for work-release and post-release employment."

- "Provide a centralized city-wide employment service to bridge the gap between imprisonment and job placement upon release."

- "Utilize available manpower funds (federal, state and local) to develop large-scale public employment programs aimed at permanent civil service status."

- "Organize all existing public and voluntary programs into a comprehensive system to coordinate job development activity through pooled resources."

- "Give special consideration to the employment of people with criminal convictions in job-development, placement and training of prisoners and other people with criminal convictions and to staffing special units within the State Employment Service and the Department of Social Services for people with criminal convictions" (CNYCHR, 1972)

Some of these recommendations were acted upon in Governor Carey's 1976 legislative program. However, overall, only a few of the commission's recommendations were adopted. Considering the state of Black unemployment in New York City today, it would be criminal for our state not to address the problems facing people with criminal convictions. Given the current economic crisis, we need to initiate comprehensive legislation that goes beyond comparable laws in other states. New York State should be the very first to implement a system of spent sentences legislation for most crimes, nonviolent and violent alike, because people who have committed violent crimes will be a part of society whether we like it or not. Do we want people who are capable of violent behavior walking our streets with nothing to lose because they are unemployed?

The ultimate goal should be to rehabilitate people with criminal convictions and reintroduce them into normal, law-abiding society. We do not live in the Dark Ages. New York State could set the standard for other states to follow. This would take courage.

The Coalition for Criminal Justice Reform (CCJR), a group that includes several nonprofit agencies that advocate for people with criminal convictions, released a report called "Blueprint for Criminal Justice Reform: Bringing Justice to Scale." Page thirty-six of that document, under the section "Second Chance," reads:

> Recognizing the wisdom of assisting individuals with criminal records to obtain employment and housing if they have completed their sentences, are qualified for employment, and are not a threat to public safety, a wide range of leaders, including a diverse group convened by former Mayor Ed Koch in 1989 and

Governor Pataki when he proposed his drug law reform bill of 2003, have proposed that New York State enact a "Second Chance" law to permit the sealing of certain nonviolent criminal records. Building on their proposals and consultations with Mayor Koch and a wide range of policymakers and experts, the Legal Action Center has drafted a bill to give qualified people with criminal records a Second Chance to achieve the American dream of a productive, self-sufficient life for themselves and their families (CCJR, 2007).

With all due respect to the great works of the Legal Action Center and CCJR, which includes many noted and justly honored organizations, Their "Blueprint for Criminal Justice Reform: Bringing Justice to Scale" report is dangerous and discriminatory. It suggests that violent offenders and their families should suffer the punishment of civil death penalties permanently.

First of all, it is a conflict of interest for any nonprofit organization with a mission of providing assistance and advocacy to people with criminal convictions to endorse legislation that will only help people with nonviolent criminal convictions and leave all others to simply die or go back to jail.

Secondly, violent offenders have a harder time finding employment compared to nonviolent offenders. In other studies, it was found that employers were more favorable toward hiring nonviolent offenders than violent ones.

Thirdly, according to Congressman Charles Rangel, the CCJR, and many other prominent advocacy groups, the purpose of second-chance legislation is to give people with criminal convictions a real second chance; to avoid well-documented discrimination from employers. The goal is to remove the social stigma attached to a criminal conviction. This would allow former offenders the opportunity (depending on individual efforts toward rehabilitation) to put their past behind them. Are these groups saying that *all* violent offenders can never be rehabilitated?

Punishment for crimes should be reserved for police, courts, and correctional facilities. Not all people with criminal convictions can be (or even desire to be) rehabilitated. However, if a person with a criminal conviction has paid their debt to society, is living a law-abiding life; has waited a reasonable amount of time after their release from incarceration or probation supervision, it is unfair and irresponsible to deny that person the opportunity to put their past behind them, even if (as in the case of some people with violent offenses) more time is needed for them to prove their worth.

If advocates for people with criminal convictions are themselves discriminating against formerly convicted people, how can these same advocates expect employers or anyone else to treat them? Advocates of people with criminal convictions are not in any position to ask employers to give violent offenders a second chance when they themselves do not afford such leniency. This is why second-chance legislation in its present form is simply wrong, unfair, unrighteous, and narrow-minded.

Level heads must prevail in this matter, for the best interest of everyone involved. A legitimate second-chance policy could dramatically reduce crime in the coming decades. We have to question the conventional wisdom and intentions of our leaders regarding to crime and punishment. Second-class-citizen status for former offenders should not be tolerated under any circumstances.

CHAPTER

11

SHOULD FORMERLY CONVICTED PEOPLE BE CONSIDERED A PROTECTED CLASS?

There are over 16 million people with criminal convictions in the United States. Title VII of the Civil Rights Act of 1964 prohibits employment discrimination based on race, color, religion, sex, or national origin. A criminal background should be added to Title VII's list of potential grounds for discrimination. This portion of the population has grown every year for the past thirty years.

The Constitution of the United States should be amended to include people with criminal convictions as a protected group. America protects every other comparable group. How could the Founding Fathers have foreseen that in the year 2009 there would be over 16 million people with criminal convictions in America, a majority of whom are Black? The Constitution does not address civil death penalties, and its framers surely could not have foreseen the innovations that allow the dissemination of criminal background information over the Internet. The Thirteenth and Fourteenth Amendments to the Constitution did not foresee the problems that people with criminal convictions would face in a technologically advanced society that is constantly exposed to media portrayals of Blacks as violent criminals.

Popular television shows like *L.A. Law, Cops, Cold Case Files, Law & Order, NYPD Blue, American Justice* and the *CSI* series offer a daily dose of negative portrayals, frequently depicting Blacks involved in criminal behavior. This creates an unfavorable perception of Blacks to the public.

> We know from the results of field experiments that employers consistently avoid Black workers, hiring them at roughly half the rate of equally qualified whites. Where models of statistical discrimination might interpret this behavior as the rational response to observed differences in the productivity of Black and white workers, the present research questions this conclusion. The majority of employers who report positive experiences with Black workers (or no differences between Black and white workers) nevertheless maintain strong negative attitudes about Black men generally (Pager and Karafin, 2009).

Blacks are far behind whites in every field of endeavor. One reason for this is that whites had a two-century-plus head start economically. Secretary of State Condoleezza Rice has stated:

> Black Americans were a founding popu-
> lation. Africans and Europeans came here
> and founded this country together …
> Europeans by choice and Africans in
> chains. That's not a very pretty reality of
> our founding, as a result, descendants of
> slaves did not get much of a head start,
> and I think you continue to see some of
> the effects of that (Kralov, 2008).

The racial discrimination in hiring shown in the Princeton study reveals a dirty little secret about hidden prejudices—as well as preferences many whites (and other non-Blacks) feel toward employing Blacks. Blacks, more than any other group, have had to bear the burden of underclass status from the very founding of America. The Thirteenth and Fourteenth Amendments to the Constitution did not equal the playing field between whites and Blacks, nor did they guarantee economic parity between them. Blacks did not achieve full political power until the Voting Rights Act of 1965.

President Lyndon B. Johnson and Congress came to the conclusion that the existing laws against racial discrimination were insufficient in compelling individual states to obey the Fifteenth Amendment, covering the right of all eligible citizens to vote. We find ourselves facing a similar problem today, with people with criminal convictions striving to acquire employment.

Different states used different tactics in denying Blacks the right to vote, the same way different states use different approaches to deny people with criminal convictions the right to be treated fairly while seeking employment. Fighting discrimination on a state-by-state, case-by-case basis is a failing proposition. The very moment one form of discrimination is uncovered and struck down by a court; another form of discrimination is created.

This was why federal intervention was necessary in the sixties, and it is also why federal intervention is overdue now to bridge the gap between the haves and have-nots of our time. The difference between the sixties and now is the absence of strong civil rights leadership. Last year we observed the fortieth anniversary of the assassination of the Reverend Dr. Martin Luther King, Jr. This year we inaugurated the first African-American President of the United States of America. We certainly have come a long way from the grim days of segregation and Jim Crow.

However, Blacks and other minorities still face barriers to employment and housing. Blacks have held— and currently hold—some of the most prestigious and powerful positions in this country. However, Black people cannot rise to equality until the entire history of discrimination in this country; as well as its effects on generations of Black families, is taken into account.

Even with discrimination being less overt now, Blacks still are plagued by it wherever they go in this country. Black people with criminal convictions have been vilified in this country to a point where several decades of reeducation and therapy are needed to heal the deep-seated wounds. Discriminatory hiring practices inflict financial hardships on people with criminal convictions and their families all across this nation.

America is in an economic downturn of historic measures. The subprime mortgage crisis and financial-industry collapse have severely affected our economy. The Federal Reserve is giving multi-billion-dollar bailouts to banks and financial institutions collapsing under the brutal weight of mortgage and credit crises. Former President George W. Bush and his successor, President Obama, approved stimulus packages aimed at jump-starting our economy.

As a result of globalization, jobs previously held by American citizens have moved overseas. A total lack of oversight by the federal government has allowed mortgage brokers to profit from bad loans made to unsuspecting families in search of the American dream. In the looming recession, people with criminal convictions will suffer unacceptable financial and economic hardships. Even college graduates are finding it hard to land employment in the present economy.

The wealth disparity between Blacks and whites has not changed much since the signing of the Civil Rights Act of 1964. In a recent report by the Institute for Policy Studies (IPS) called "40 Years Later: The Unrealized American Dream," a disturbing trend is documented. The survey found that while high school and college graduation rates have improved since 1968, "it will take more than 537 more years for Blacks to reach income equality with Whites if the income gap continues to close at the same rate it has since Dr. King was assassinated." The report goes on to state that, forty years after Martin Luther King, Jr. called for an end to poverty, "the annual decline of poverty for Black children is about a quarter of a percentage point per year. At this rate it will take over a century to end poverty for Black children. Today a third of Black children live in poverty" (Muhammed, 2008).

The IPS report exposed an undeniable truth about race relations in this country that must be addressed with all deliberate speed. The truth is Black Americans have unjustly been made to bear the burden of poverty in America, while many whites have enjoyed economic prosperity based on racial privilege. The IPS report proves with shocking clarity that Title VII of the Civil Rights Act of 1964 has *failed* to protect Blacks from unfair discriminatory practices.

The recent economic discoveries highlighted in the IPS report coupled with the large population of American citizens with criminal convictions shows that the laws passed in the sixties for the purpose of creating a level economic playing field have been for the most part unsuccessful. The Constitution has been amended several times to bring relief to the American citizenry in the past.

The Constitution, while a well intentioned document written by some of the greatest minds in the history of America, is not a "walking document," (a document that could evolve on its own to fit the changing times, situations, and demographics of America). Nor is it a perfect document. The provisions of the Constitution have to be revisited from time to time to bring the document in line with the changing economic times, complex social situations (such as civil death penalties), and the changing racial demographics of our country. Selfishness, greed, hate, discrimination, ignorance, and inertia on the part of citizens of all races and genders have fermented and refined the unemployment problem facing American citizens with criminal convictions.

Title VII of the Civil Rights Act of 1964 should be amended to protect people previously convicted of criminal offenses from unreasonable discrimination in seeking employment. Taking into account the size of this population group, people with criminal convictions should be considered a separate and distinct class or group as with gender, age, race, creed, or national origin. People with criminal convictions should be added to that list of groups that are historically ostracized and face discrimination in employment, housing, and other areas.

By implementing spent sentence policies to people with criminal convictions; and reintroducing them into society as whole citizens, we would solve several crucial social problems. We would save the tax dollars that would be spent on incarceration of recidivists, on building facilities and hiring officers and staff used to house and police this population. We also would reduce crime and lessen the victimization of our citizens. The criminal justice system in New York State, which is comprised of mostly upstate New York residents profiting from the criminalization and victimization of mostly New York City residents, is a scavenger industry.

Currently New York State leaves the burden of proof of discrimination to the previously convicted. One of the great misconceptions of Certificates of Relief from Disabilities and Certificates of Good Conduct is that possession of such a certificate is sufficient to shift burden of proof to employers in proving discrimination. This is generally not the case. If an applicant is denied employment because of a criminal conviction, the applicant has to file a case by way of an Article 78 proceeding to why that denial was in violation to Article 23-A of the Corrections Law. Thus, the person with the criminal conviction is not only denied employment, but must sue the potential employer to prove that they were discriminated against.

If the burden of proof was truly placed on the employer, then the employer (not the applicant) would have to file suit to prove that the person with the criminal conviction is unsafe for employment. This would mean that the applicant would have to be granted employment until a decision is made by the courts; and the person's criminal offense made them an *unreasonable risk* to the employer's business interests.

An Article 78 proceeding is not only complicated for most individuals, such a proceeding entails legal expenses and takes several months at the least. Every other large group in America is protected under Title VII of the Civil Rights Act of 1964. Civil death penalties affect Blacks by almost a three-to-one margin. The social stigma placed on this group, coupled with the racial disparities in conviction rates, along with the slow economy, makes it a must that our federal government intervenes. People with criminal convictions are clearly at a disadvantage when applying for employment, especially in a crowded labor marketplace.

When it was shown that women were being discriminated against in the work place; the federal government intervened to protect them. When it was found that employers were discriminating against older citizens, the federal government intervened. When employers discriminated on grounds of religious faith; the federal government intervened to end the discrimination. Employers discriminated against applicants based on their skin color, creed or national origin. The federal government intervened. When the right to vote was denied to women and Blacks, the federal government intervened (eventually).

Now that we know that people with criminal convictions are openly being discriminated against by employers, creditors, and licensing agencies, the federal government must intervene by amending Title VII of the Civil Rights Act of 1964 to include people with criminal convictions as a group or class that must be protected from unfair, unreasonable, and unjust discrimination. It is simply unacceptable for our government, with all of the information available on the problems people with criminal convictions are having, to allow these penalties to continue any longer. One of the measures we need to take is amending the public biographies of formerly convicted people after they have proved their rehabilitation. The leprosy-like stigma legally placed on the public records of people with criminal convictions is an uncivilized practice that should be reserved for active criminal offenders.

There are several different models for New York State to follow. Second-chance legislation in its present form is an ineffective and narrow-minded solution to a very serious problem. Simply funding nonprofits and faith-based organizations is tantamount to placing a Band-Aid over a flat tire. It will *not* work, and we have over 30 years of proof to this fact.

This is not to say that more funding is not needed to expand the very limited services for people with criminal convictions. This is certainly not to disparage these organizations that have offered much-needed services to our communities. But the problem lies in the social stigma and discrimination, not in the approach of these agencies.

NYSDOCS provides prisoners with pre-release counseling and other necessary services before they are considered fit for discharge into society. Nonprofit organizations provide re-entry services, including job training, job search preparation, and housing assistance (an issue of growing importance in expensive, crowded New York City). But assistance to former offenders should focus on the psychological problems caused by prolonged sojourns in violent correctional institutions. The only way that we can effectively tackle the growing problems people with criminal convictions have finding employment is to implement innovative legislation that would reduce or eliminate employment disparities.

CHAPTER

12

HOW TO END UNFAIR DISCRIMINATORY PRACTICES AGAINST THE FORMERLY CONVICTED

Posturing, fear tactics, and highly public incidents are common processes by which political careers are started and advanced in New York State and the rest of the country. Politicians often use high-profile crimes to call for sweeping legislation that will punish criminal offenders more harshly and incarcerate them longer. What New York State needs desperately is for all major supporters of civil consequences reform to stand together and demand from our elected officials that they differentiate active criminals from previously convicted people. Our state government must be as willing to reward rehabilitated people by relieving them of civil death penalties as they are to punish active criminal offenders. New York State has a chance to take the lead nationally in treating former offenders fairly.

New York State only has to make minor revisions in policy to reduce the discrimination formerly convicted people face as a result of their conviction. Here are three changes to our current Correction and Civil Rights laws that, if implemented, could reduce crime, substantially lower the cost of incarcerating criminal offenders, and ultimately make our communities safer. Although we must also provide better educational institutions for minority children and parents must play a more positive role in the upbringing of their children, these revisions should bring instant relief to our communities:

1. AMEND ARTICLE 23-A OF THE CORRECTION LAW

In order to precipitate the employment of people with criminal convictions, we need to amend the public biography of people with criminal convictions once a graduated rehabilitation has been achieved. Several studies show conclusively that employers are not willing to hire people with criminal convictions. Employers must be denied disparaging information at the beginning of the job application process. The problem with employers considering past offenses when hiring is simply that employers are human beings. Employers (as with all humans) are subject to opinions and biases that prevent them from being fair and reasonable when it comes to hiring formerly incarcerated people.

Article 23-A of the Correction Law as it now stands is clearly ineffective in preventing discrimination based on past criminal offenses. First, Certificates of Relief from Disabilities and Certificates of Good Conduct only give a "presumption of rehabilitation." What "presumption" means in this legislation is largely unclear. How many years must a person with criminal convictions abstain from criminal behavior before he or she is considered rehabilitated? Certificates of Rehabilitation can be obtained at sentencing from the sentencing judge. This is why the actual character of the person receiving the certificate is unclear and risky for employers to put faith in. Furthermore, the Certificate of Relief from Disabilities is truly unnecessary because the Certificate of Good Conduct does exactly the same thing and restores the right to hold public office. Both certificates relieve the statutory bars to employment, and both require a background investigation into work history and personal references. Having these two certificates that essentially do the same thing is only an exercise in bureaucratic waste. If a formerly convicted person receives a sentence that does not contain incarceration, a certificate from the sentencing judge relieving "automatic bars" to employment should be unnecessary, since the sentencing judge and the prosecuting attorney did not see a need to remove the offender from the community. There should not be automatic bars to employment for offenders not deemed threats to society.

The Certificate of Good Conduct is actually the more trusted certificate. Even though a person has to wait five years after sentencing (in the case of a sentence that does not contain incarceration) or five years after release from incarceration, this time gives the Division of Parole a chance to assess the public, work, and civic records of the person applying for the certificate.

The obvious conclusion to reforming Article 23-A of the Correction Law would be to add a "Certificate of Rehabilitation" to be awarded after eight years of acceptable conduct on the part of the formerly convicted person. The Certificate of Rehabilitation would entitle the person to have the charge(s) the certificate covers to be sealed, set aside, pardoned, or expunged from the public record.

Ultimately, employers are a part of society. New York is overburdening most minority communities with thousands of unemployed people with criminal convictions who may see no other way to support themselves and their families except through criminal activities. States and employers have the responsibility of protecting their interests. New York State's interest is the safety and protection of its citizenry and an employer's interest is the growth of their business, and the safety of their customers and employees.

Recent legislation has removed the risk of negligent hiring lawsuits against employers who abide by Article 23-A of the Correction Law and hire people with criminal convictions. Equally important is the fact that employers would not be less responsible for criminal incidents on the job if the offender in question has no criminal record.

There are mountains of statistical data that shows lack of employment raises crime rates. Amending Article 23-A of the Correction Law to incorporate a Certificate of Rehabilitation after eight years of successful rehabilitative effort by the person with a criminal conviction would serve two major purposes. First, employers would be protected against negligent hiring charges, because once a person with a criminal conviction receives the Certificate of Rehabilitation, the employer enjoys protection from the State of New York. Second, our communities will be less burdened with criminal behavior when people with criminal convictions are productively and legally employed.

The same standard of investigation would apply to the Certificate of Rehabilitation as the Certificate of Good Conduct. Remove the Certificate of Relief from Disabilities altogether. Employment barriers should not be placed on criminal offenders that are not a threat to society.

2. CREATE A CRIMINAL OFFENDER INFORMATION BOARD

The purpose of the Criminal Offender Information Board (COIB) is to protect people with criminal convictions from unreasonable job discrimination by requiring employers to apply to a board of professionals trained in the field of criminology and job discrimination. The COIB will have access to all criminal conviction information and will decide the relevance of a person's criminal offense to the job they are applying for. Modeled after the Massachusetts board process, this would remove the burden of proof from both people with criminal convictions and employers, and place that burden on the state. New York must bear some responsibility for the social stigma it has placed on criminal offenders. Presently, the State of New York allows employers to d*eny first, and answer questions later.*

What the Massachusetts legislation does is limit the information employers can request on a job application,

Eric M. Deadwiley

which makes perfect sense, particularly in New York State where both the incarceration and unemployment rates of young Black males are very high.

A program like this would help in several different areas. First, it would cut down on unnecessary litigation. Secondly, the COIB could compile data on how many people with criminal convictions are actively seeking employment; as well as the outcomes of their searches. Thirdly, our economy would grow due to increased employment of Black males previously shut out from gainful labor. Fourth, the cost of operating the COIB would be minuscule in comparison to existing expenditures on incarceration, welfare, indigent litigant fees, and the social costs of victimization.

Last but certainly not least, the COIB would balance the business interest of employers with the civil rights of people with criminal convictions as they seek to close the door on their past and move forward with their lives. We currently have state agencies that have the capacity to operate the COIB as a subsidiary department.

The Equal Employment Opportunities Commission and the Division of Human Rights not only have the capacity to operate such a board, but they have fully trained officers and investigators who are knowledgeable on discriminatory practices and their effects on our communities—an invaluable set of working knowledge. At present, New York allows employers who have no training whatsoever in the field of criminology or character profiling to attempt to make decisions about people with criminal convictions and their chances of relapsing.

CIVIL DEATH IN NEW YORK STATE

Our state allows employers to make subjective decisions about people with criminal convictions mostly based on their *personal ideologies*. Employers should not be allowed to make these decisions alone. New York State is one of the worst violators of formerly incarcerated people's civil and human rights. Yet New York State has a chance to take the lead in implementing rehabilitation legislation.

New York State has the organizational structure already in place to assume this responsibility. New York State should "ban the box" on most public and private employment applications, the "box" being the question on most job applications that requests conviction information. Ban the dissemination of this information to and from online information service providers such as Intellius. Create a Criminal Offender Information Board to protect the business interests of employers *and* provide the privacy, economic opportunity, and legal protection that people with criminal convictions and their families deserve.

3. SEAL CONVICTIONS AFTER TEN YEARS OF PROVEN REHABILITATION

With over 16 million people with criminal convictions in the United States, a number which grows exponentially each year, many advocates are calling for a time limit to be placed on public access to rehabilitated people's criminal background information. With the economic forecast looking bleak at best, we need to make substantial changes in how we apply civil death penalties to our citizenry. A

Eric M. Deadwiley

growing number of community activist, politicians, and academics are openly calling for formerly convicted people to be given a second chance to rehabilitate themselves.

The main opponents of restricting information to the public have been employers. Their central argument is that they are subject to negligent hiring suits if they hire a person with a criminal conviction and that person commits a crime on the job. They wrongfully assert that the threat of negligent hiring suits exist even if the employer is following the law by not discriminating against qualified people with criminal convictions whose crime is not related to the job sought. A first step in easing the concerns about hiring people with criminal convictions is to protect employers who follow the law and desist from discriminating. A new law sponsored by Assemblymen Aubry et al, amended the Human Rights Law to "create a rebuttable presumption in favor of excluding evidence of an employee's past criminal record in a negligent hiring case where the employer has complied with Article 23-A of the Correction Law" (Aubry, 2008). This law is a major step toward integrating formerly convicted people into normal society.

This law also sets the stage for removing criminal record information from public scrutiny after rehabilitation has been achieved. Accessing criminal background information for non-criminal purposes must end at some point. Not only do these tough-on-crime penalties disparately impact Black families, studies have shown conclusively that these laws have advanced the unemployment rates in the communities with the highest concentrations of people with criminal convictions, which are more often than not, Black and Latino communities.

Blacks have a hard enough time finding employment without the stigma of a criminal background. Blacks do not control the businesses and institutions in their communities. This often leaves Blacks with no other alternative than to rely on others to employ them, others that may have hiring preferences toward people they may feel more comfortable with which oftentimes are people of their own national, religious, and cultural background, as well as their own race. Racism is still a problem in New York State. This is why many advocates are pushing for second-chance legislation that is reasonable. Another good model for New York State to follow is Hawaii's Employment Practices Act, HRS Section 378-2.5, which limits certain employers' consideration of criminal background information to offenses that occurred within the past ten years. Hawaii's Section 378-2.5 (c) reads:

> For purposes of this section, "conviction" means an adjudication by a court of competent jurisdiction that the defendant committed a crime, not including final judgments required to be confidential pursuant to section 571-84; provided that the employer may consider the employee's conviction record falling within a period that shall not exceed the most recent ten years, excluding periods of incarceration (University of Hawaii, 2008).

The law also requires that employers give a conditional offer of employment before determining whether a person's criminal offense is in some way related to the job sought. Requiring employers to give a conditional offer of employment before obtaining criminal background information should be a part of Article 23-A of the Correction Law, because employers frequently avoid challenges of their discriminatory practices by simply denying employment to people with criminal convictions for other reasons.

The San Francisco Human Rights Commission passed a resolution sponsored by All of Us or None, a project of Legal Services for Prisoners with Children, urging the State of California and other smaller government entities to eliminate the box on public applications requiring disclosure of past criminal offenses. All of Us or None has been in the forefront of the "ban the box" movement.

The box containing the question "Have you ever been convicted of a crime?"—is a malicious attempt to deny previously convicted people employment. The antiquity of the offense is rarely considered. Employers do not take into account the children of the person with criminal convictions—some who may not have been born at the time the offense occurred. For a human to prevent a dog from feeding its puppies would be looked upon as savage and cruel behavior. The cognitive dissidence our political representative's exhibit to maintain such archaic penalties is astonishing. It takes you a step further into their pathologies about crime, punishment, and race.

Criminal convictions should be sealed from public scrutiny after ten years of rehabilitative efforts have been achieved. As also recognized by Hawaii, ten years is a reasonable amount of time for formerly convicted people to prove that they no longer are involved in criminal activities. Ten years should be the limitation on allowing people with criminal convictions to be legally discriminated against by employers. Within those ten years, Article 23-A of the Correction Law can serve as a benchmark for what a person must achieve before earning the opportunity to seal their criminal record. With minor revisions to Article 23-A to incorporate an actual Certificate of Rehabilitation after eight years of proven rehabilitation, New York can effectively promote public safety and civil rights at the same time.

The Certificate of Relief from Disabilities should be removed altogether. Five years should be the minimum requirement for a certificate if these certificates are going to serve as some form of indicator or "presumption of rehabilitation."

The former offender must obtain the Certificate of Rehabilitation to seal their criminal record from public scrutiny. Nonviolent drug offender sentences should become spent after five years of successful rehabilitative efforts and obtainment of the Certificate of Good Conduct. All other offenses should become automatically spent after ten years of rehabilitative efforts and obtainment of both the Certificate of Good Conduct and Certificate of Rehabilitation.

In Closing

For over forty years, politicians and advocates for formerly convicted people have been unsuccessful in getting legislation passed that would do away with the social stigma a criminal conviction carries. As a result, the prison-industrial complex has grown to an inconceivable size. The prison-industrial complex is a scavenger industry. It feeds off our citizen's physical bodies.

The explosion of the prison-industrial complex is a product of crime, victimization, and despair. Without crime and victimization, hundreds of jobs would be lost in upstate facilities, and in rural and suburban towns where the residents are not the victims of the criminal behavior centered in urban communities. This is at the center of the resistance to true legislative change that will remove unreasonable bars to employment for millions of people with criminal convictions in New York State. Just minor changes in policy will actually close many of these upstate prisons, ultimately saving the state millions in expenditures. These three legislative changes should be implemented with all deliberate speed. These changes will protect the civil and human rights of people with criminal convictions, while at the same time protecting the business interest of employers. These proposals will protect employers from unfair negligent hiring suits. Furthermore, these proposals make all the parties involved in the rehabilitation of formerly convicted people equally responsible for their successful reintegration into society.

The stigma of a criminal background cannot be a lifetime disability in modern civilized society. We cannot make the same mistakes of the past. We cannot settle for ineffective legislative reform that will maintain the prison-industrial complex in upstate New York as it presently exists.

The idea of spent sentences is not new. The problem is that policies such as spent sentencing and sealing criminal records through expunction have been discriminately applied. Most states that allow the sealing of criminal offenses only allow nonviolent offenses to be sealed. Yet nonviolent offenders are not the only offenders who must support themselves and their dependents. An argument can be made that nonviolent offenders should be awarded the relief sooner than violent offenders. However, for any politician or advocate to suggest (like Congressman Charles Rangel did) that *only* nonviolent offenders should be relieved from the social stigma of a criminal record for employment purposes while allowing those who have committed violent offenses to be forever ostracized from society is wrong as well as dangerous.

Canada and Hawaii are good models other states could follow in the hopes of lessening their crime problem. New York State has major economic issues that could be solved by untying the hands of tens of thousands of rehabilitated people with criminal convictions who are needlessly discriminated against by employers. The Canadian and Hawaiian models have the potential of pumping needed tax revenue into our state. The time for reasonable reform of our felony disenfranchisement laws is now.

Let us not miss another opportunity to do the right thing. Whatever dignity and self-esteem that was not striped away from an individual while incarcerated is most certainly ripped away when they have to beg and plead for a job. We need to limit civil death penalties for rehabilitated people with criminal convictions so that they may close the door on their past and move on with their lives. In the final analysis, even formerly convicted people must have an income to feed their families, and they need to be able to contribute to society. This will help them redeem themselves. Many of us have done something wrong in our lives, something that we are ashamed of. Yet because of forgiving people willing to give second chances, many of us was able to fulfill our dreams. Even President Barack Obama admitted as much to the nation:

> ...I wasn't always as focused as I should have been. I did some things I'm not proud of, and got in more trouble than I should have. And my life could have easily taken a turn for the worse. But I was fortunate. I got a lot of second chances and had the opportunity to go to college, and law school, and follow my dreams (Associated Press, 2009).

If the New York State Legislature is not willing or able to work in a bipartisan way to remove unreasonable bars to fair employment of people with prior convictions, a class-action lawsuit should be filed on behalf of people with criminal convictions and their dependents against the State of New York. These policies have had a disparate and disastrous impact on Black families all across the state. Judicial intervention on the Federal or International level may be required

BIBLIOGRAPHY

"An act to amend the correction law and the executive law, in relation to establishing that it is an unlawful discriminatory practice for prospective employers to make certain inquiries relating to criminal convictions." New York State Assembly, February 2009 (Aubry J. , 2009).

"An act to amend the Correction Law and the executive law in relation to the removal of disabilities of criminal offenders and repealing certain provisions thereof. Article 23-A of the New York State Corrections Law § 296 Article 15 of the Human Rights Law" New York State Assembly, July 1976.

"An act to amend the criminal procedure law and the executive law, in relation to the conditional sealing of drug convictions." New York State Assembly, May 2006 (Aubry A. J., 2006).

"An act to amend the executive law in relation to evidence of an employee's past criminal record." New York State AssemblyError! Hyperlink reference not valid., July 2008.

Anderson, C. *Black Labor White Wealth*. Bethesda, Maryland: PowerNomics Corporation, 1994.

Associated Press. "Prepared text of Obama's speech to school students." Yahoo! News. http://news.yahoo.com/s/ap/20090907/ap_on_go_pr_wh/us_obama_school_speech_text/pr...

Boothe, D. *Why Are So Many Black Men In Prison?* Full Surface Publishing, 2007

Bowles, Jonathan. *Reviving the City of Aspiration: A Study of the Challenges Facing New York City's Middle Class.* New York: Center for an Urban Future, 2009.

Coalition for Criminal Justice Reform. "Blueprint for Criminal Justice Reform- Bringing Justice to Scale." Legal Action Center. http://www.lac.org/pub/gratis/Blueprint_final_11-29-06.pdf (accessed March 24, 2008).

City of New York Commission on Human Rights. "The Employment Problems of Ex-offenders. New York: City of New York Commission on Human Rights, 1972.

DePalma, Brian (director). *Scarface*. Motion picture, 1983.

Encyclopedia Britannica, 2009. S.v. "Corporal punishment."

Gershman, J. "Putting Sex Predators in Mental Facilities May Impact Plea Bargains. *New York Sun*, 10 February 2006.

Hammond, B. "A Crackhead for your kid. Albany must repeal law that hides daycare workers' drug records." *New York Daily News*, 26 May 2009.

Huffington Post. "Obama 100 Days Press Conference." April 29, 2009, http://www.huffingtonpost.com/2009/04/29/ obam-100-days--press-conf_n_193283.html.

Levine, Harry, G. *The Marijuana Arrest Crusade in New York City.* New York: NYCLU, 2008.

Joffe, Ronald. (director). *The Scarlet Letter.* Motion picture, 1995.King,

Jr., Martin Luther. *The Trumpet of Conscience.* New York: Harper and Row, 1967.

Karafin, Diana. "Bayesian Bigot? Statistical Discrimination, Stereotyping, and Employer Decision Making." *Annals of the American Academy of Political and Social Science*, 621 (2009): 70-93.

Kralov, Nicholas. "Rice hits U.S. 'birth defect'." *Washington Times*, 2008.

Megan Kurlychek, Robert Brame & Shawn D. Bushway. "Scarlet Letters and Recidivism: Does an Old Criminal Record Predict Future Offending?" *Reentry Policy* 5-3 (2006): 1101-1122.

Lathan, Stan (director). *Dave Chapelle: Killin' Them Softly.* Motion picture, 2000.

Levitan, Mark. *Unemployment and Joblessness in New York City, 2006.* New York: The Community Service Society, 2007.

Maddox, Jr., Alton H. 2008. "A criticism of Black politics." *New York Amsterdam News*, 12.

Morrow, Alvin. *Breaking The Curse Of Willie Lynch.* Florissant, Missouri: Rising Sun Publications, 2003.

Muhammed, Dedrick. *40 Years Later: The Unrealized American Dream.* Washington, D.C.: Institute for Policy Studies, 2008.

Nagin, Ray. Interview by Tavis Smiley, 22 February 2008.

National Consortium for Justice Information and Statistics. *United States Survey of State Criminal History Information Systems, 2006*, 2008.

New York State Department of Correctional Services. "An Analysis of the Impact of Prison Program Participation on Community Success." 2007.

New York State Department of Correctional Services. "Three Year Post Release Follow-Up." 2002.

New York State Department of Correctional Services. "The Departmental Mission." 2009.

New York State Division of Human Rights. "Protections Under the Human Rights Law for People Convicted of Criminal Offenses." http://www.dhr.state.ny.us.

Pager, Devah. "Race At Work." Department of Sociology, Princeton University, 2005.

Pager, Devah. "The Mark of a Criminal Record." *American Journal of Sociology* (2003), 956.

Pinkerton, J. "Crime and Punishment in Colonial America." eSSORTMENT. http://ohoh.essortment. com/colonialpunishm_rkzt.htm.

Post, Ted. (director). *Hang 'Em High*. Motion picture, 1968.

Rangel, Charles B. "The Second Chance Act of 2007." United States House of Representatives. http://thomas. loc.gov/cgi-bin/query/D?c1101:./temp/~c110wi3a2U::.

Rogers, G. M., director. *March of the Wooden Soldiers*. Motion picture, 1934.

Rick Ruddell and Thomas Winfree, Jr. 2006. "Setting Aside Criminal Convictions in Canada." *The Prison Journal* , 465-466.

United States Census Bureau. "U.S. Census Bureau Guidance on the Presentation and Comparison of Race and Hispanic Origin Data." United States Census Bureau. http://www.census.gov/population/www/socdemo/ compraceho.html (accessed June 12, 2006).

United States Department of Labor. "Labor-Management Reporting and Disclosure Act of 1959" Employment Standards Administration, Office of Labor-Management Standards. http://www.dol.gov/esa (accessed May 9, 2007).

United States Immigration Support. "Illegal Immigration to the United States." United States Immigration Support. http://www.usimmigrationsupport.org/articles_illegal_ immigration.html (accessed September 5, 2009).

University of Hawaii. "HRS Chapter 378, Hawaii's Employment Practices Act." Center For Labor Education Research. http://homepages.uhwo.hawaii.edu/~clear/HRS378.html (accessed September 10, 2009).

Webster's Ninth New Collegiate Dictionary. Springfield: Merriam-Webster Inc., 2009.